I AM FREE

*Healing stories about
surviving toxic relationships
with narcissists and sociopaths*

Bree Bonchay, LCSW

Book cover design by Ellie Bockert Augsburger of Creative Digital Studios. www.CreativeDigitalStudios.com

Cover design features: fiery phoenix: © jjordanov / Dollar Photo Club

DEDICATION

To everyone whose life has been adversely impacted by a narcissist or sociopath, I dedicate this book to you. I hope you will find it a source of comfort and an instrument of hope and a constant reminder that you deserve to live a life filled with love, happiness, peace, and FREEDOM.

CONTENTS

ACKNOWLEDGMENTS

THIS BOOK WOULD NOT HAVE been possible without the contribution and support of so many people whom I have had the good fortunate to get to know throughout this endeavor. I want to express my deepest gratitude to everyone who submitted their stories to this project. Your words of encouragement, messages of support, and desire to help others have meant so much to me and truly embody the vision I had for *I Am Free*.

I also want to thank my very insightful daughter, who is my inspiration, for all her patience, help, and understanding during all those times I was glued to the computer.

And thank you and big hugs to my biggest supporters, Richie, Marcia Graeber, Julie Aguayo, Laura Jagielo and Mommie Dianne, who have encouraged me and believed in me every step of the way along this journey.

I would like to thank Kevin Anderson and Associates for editing, proofreading and guidance.

Thank you to Ellie Kay Bosckert Augsburger at Creative Digital Studios for the beautiful cover design and layout that was chosen as the favorite by the Narcissistic Abuse and Toxic Relationship Forum members.

And thank you to the forum members who provided their input and helped decide which cover would best represent the message of this book.

INTRODUCTION

WE HAVE BEEN IN THE same place as you.

We have drowned in our own confusion. We have felt lost in our hopelessness and alone in our anguish. We have weathered the soul-shattering pain of betrayal and the shock of being on the receiving end of a soul that lacks empathy.

We have ignored our intuition and the little nagging voices in our heads because we couldn't bring ourselves to believe an incomprehensible truth: a truth that was unimaginable and too painful to bear.

We suffocated under the crushing weight of a one-sided relationship. We were plagued with bouts of unremitting self-doubt. "Is it us?" "Or is it them?" We accepted the blame for things that we knew weren't our fault. We walked on eggshells and censored what we said to keep the peace. We slowly became drained and weakened with every act of insidious cruelty, only to have our hopes falsely restored through fleeting glimpses of what once was. We have scoured the Internet searching for an explanation to help us understand our loved one's behavior. We abandoned ourselves while trying to love the one person who was incapable of loving us in return.

We, the former partners and ex spouses, the children and siblings and friends and employees of narcissists and sociopaths, understand what you're going through.

That is why we feel compelled to share our stories. To speak out about our experiences in hopes that others will recognize the similar threads of malice, and the warning signs that we disregarded or did not know to be warning signs at the time.

We don't want anyone else to know this place. This place that has taken many of us to the lowest depths of depression and angst. This place that so many of us believed we could never climb out of. This place of false promises and fraudulent love that never changes for the better and only gets worse through the passage time. This place of invisible wounds and deep, lingering trauma. We don't want anyone else to suffer the emotional, psychological, and oftentimes financial abuses of these personality types.

We wish we had been warned and saved from the harm inflicted upon us. No one saw the gradual and stealthy erosion of our self-esteem, our confidence, our joy, and our spirits. We even failed to recognize it, until it was too late and the damage had been done. We lived in an atmosphere constantly shifting between love and cruelty. The abuse many of us were subjected to started off gradually and more often than not, was covert and usually underneath the pretext of love and caring or just trying to be helpful.

We have felt the loneliness and silent suffering that the outside world was completely oblivious to. We have glimpsed sides of the personality disordered that are so opposite of their charming, likeable, and even quite compassionate public personas. Even many family law court judges, psychiatrists, and psycho-therapists have unknowingly failed us or dismissed our pleas for help when we so desperately needed it. They too were easily fooled because so many aren't knowledgeable or adequately trained in identifying the signs of narcissistic abuse or even addressing the aftermath of the damage caused by these toxic interactions.

We have felt the unsettling necessity to search for answers to help put the pieces of our lives back together and decode the insanity of our everyday existence.

We have spent countless hours Googling the "why does ..." questions. Why does my partner always think they're right? Why does my mother never apologize? Why does my spouse always give me the silent treatment? Why does my partner/mother/father/sibling or boss always make me feel like I'm always to blame for everything?

Our Google search queries led us to articles about narcissism. An all-pervasive pattern of behavior characterized by grandiosity, a need for admiration and lack of empathy. No, narcissism isn't limited to vanity, arrogance, and excessive selfies as most of us originally believed. It's so much more pathological and destructive than we could've ever imagined, and even worse, there is no cure.

In our search for answers, we couldn't ignore the undeniable accuracy with which the articles described our experiences. We reluctantly arrived at the devastating conclusion that we were never loved, as narcissists and sociopaths are incapable of real love and deep connection. We racked our brains, questioning and examining the validity of every good memory and every word spoken until we gradually came to accept that the person we loved was just a cleverly crafted façade that never existed.

We have seen the void where a conscience is supposed to be and witnessed the absence of the ability to feel guilt or remorse. Our compassion has been used as a weapon against us. Our love has been relentlessly exploited, only to be swiftly replaced as if we never even mattered. Our identities have been buried beneath the weight of unbalanced relationships. Our forgiveness has been abused. Our trust has been broken and our faith in humanity forever tainted. And although we are forever changed by an evil we previously never knew existed, *we are free.*

You are about to take a glimpse into the personal journeys of survivors of narcissistic abuse. Although many of the contributors' stories are raw and describe cruel and calculated acts of narcissistic abuse, you will discover that the stories are not about pain and heartache, but rather about renewed hope, lives reclaimed, and the determination to thrive. There is nothing more reassuring and encouraging than reading true stories written by real people who managed to rise from the darkest pits of despair, conquer their fears, and reclaim their power.

The *I Am Free* collection of stories and poems will inspire hope and provide comfort to you when you are dealing with the aftermath of a toxic relationship and serve as a collective cautionary tale to anyone who is in, or thinks they may be in, an emotionally abusive relationship with a narcissist or sociopath.

Since most people whose lives are impacted by the devastating effects of narcissism feel completely alone, broken, and as if no one understands the pain of what they're going through, the contributors have shared their stories offering support, messages of encouragement, and wisdom gleaned from painful lessons learned.

There is a brimming narcissistic abuse recovery community and a plethora of information on the topic of narcissism permeating the Internet and yet most survivors stumble upon these sites purely by accident. The discovery of these sites brings survivors both relief and disappointment. On one hand, many are relieved to find that there is a definitive term to explain the insanity they had been living but were previously at a loss for words to express and on the other hand, they are disappointed by the lack of preventative information being taught in schools and in society at large.

It is my hope, and the hope of every contributor, that *I Am Free* will not only bring comfort and encouragement to the survivor community but will also help to spread awareness about this growing epidemic.

In April of 2015, I founded the Narcissistic and Toxic Relationship Forum on Facebook. Over and over, I noticed survivors declaring similar versions of these three little but very powerfully liberating words—I Am Free. I wrote this book in hopes that you, too, will one day say these words.

Below are actual comments from The Narcissistic Abuse and Toxic Relationship Forum page on Facebook. The names have been changed to protect their anonymity.

"Everyone asks me how I am. No income for eight weeks now and we are going to court next week, but my answer is always the same. I am free now."

—Michelle

"I am finally free and I intend to stay that way."

—Linda

"I lost everything. My house, my job and my friends, but you can't put a price on freedom."

—Tom

"I lived with a narcissist and didn't even realize it until it was almost too late. All the signs were there. I just didn't know what they were at the time. I am free now."

—Jill

"The narcissist is delusional that his victim will always love him. Hatred comes easily to the abused and fades into indifference with time and freedom."

—Lauren

"If I had bruises on my body they would be as blue as my eyes. And so much of the time I didn't even know the abuse was happening until one day I walked away with a near empty spirit and heart, but I was free."

—Julie

"I don't understand why someone would want to tear down an amazing person that loves them. You would think they would cherish and treasure them. The more you do for them, the more they try to demean and destroy you. It makes no sense at all. Thank goodness I am free."

—Mary

"I may not have won, but that was never my objective. Sharing love was my only goal and now I do it even more. Just never with someone toxic like that again. I'm free forever."

—Matt

CHAPTER 1

WHEN THE MASK FALLS OFF

Sometimes it's not the people who change, it's the mask that falls off.
—Anonymous

PAWN BREAK

TODAY I CRIED, BUT NOT my usual tears. They were not the tears of confusion, pain and despair that I'm used to crying because of my narcissist. These were tears of relief. A sort of epiphany has rained down upon me. It's as though the weight of the world has been lifted off of my shoulders.

Everyone is keen to noticing this transformation that I'm undergoing. They notice it in my appearance, my eyes, my demeanor. This alleviation of the poison being removed from my brain has had tremendous positive effects. The toxins from a toxic person that have been slowly killing me for fourteen years are finally gone.

I took the poison willingly, while being played like a fine-tuned fiddle. It wasn't until this awakening that fourteen years of agony came crumbling down. I suddenly saw all the horror of the realities that I managed to suppress and forgive, hoping that one day the man I believed he could be, the man that I saw glimpses of, would finally arrive.

I had prayed daily and forgiven daily because I understood that he was mentally ill. He loved me in his own way. He always came back to me, so clearly it must have been me that he ultimately wanted, needed, desired, and loved. He needed to leave me and the kids to clear his head for a few months. I lived pretending things were good to everyone else, believing that one day he would "grow up."

I can detail horrific, sad stories that happened over the years and people always wonder, "Why did she stay?" The answer is that I valued his opinion of me over everyone and everything else.

I believed his mirror imaging of what I wanted to hear. I wanted to be what he needed, not what I needed and not what I was. In reality, I did not know who I was anymore. I had a deep yearning to please him, at the cost of my own soul and happiness.

Oh the stories! The cruelty, the physical, emotional, verbal abuse that I endured on a daily basis. I hid my own pain and many times bruises so that others would never think poorly of him. I loved him and was willing to protect him and his image at all costs.

He would tell everyone how crazy I was and how he couldn't deal with it, so he had to leave to go sit in bars, have parties, hang out with his friends, cheat, lie, and manipulate. He had his room set up at his mother's, phone line and cable untouched for whenever he wanted to return, as he did many times when I voiced an opinion or stood up for myself.

He wanted to put me and keep me in my place. It was too stressful for him to deal with "hearing my mouth" when he went out after work at 2:00 a.m., often turning his phone off and returning home sometimes at 5:00 a.m. Makes sense, right? After all, he had a stressful job, he was a police officer. According to him, I didn't understand the job and never would. His position gave him power. A narcissist in a powerful position is a very frightening thing.

Understanding did not come until after years of abuse. I finally asked myself, "Why am I trying to understand why he does these things?" I needed to start understanding why I stayed and allowed him to as well. Why did I allow him to feed off me and hand over my power and voice to him?

It was in this moment that clarity became reality. It was clear and painful. It was agonizing. I wept.

He wanted me with no one but him. He tried with all of his power to make sure that I was alone. I have so many amazing people who watched this for years that begged me to move on. He tried with all his might to rid these "toxic" people from me, but he was the toxin. He was that venomous snake slithering, abusing, belittling, sneaking, breaking me down to nothing. I was allowed to be in his life when it suited him; otherwise I was a nothing.

I was a pawn in his empty soul and he was looking to feed off the sparkle, the spirit, the light and the smiles that I shared with the world. When I was with him I was empty, withdrawn, sad, confused. I was his puppet, and my strings were intertwined in his hands. He played me along with every move.

As I mentioned, the clarity was painful. It was at this point that I decided to keep a journal with dates and times so that I could not be manipulated. I would no longer be accused of being confused or making events up.

I wrote everything down, including an open letter to him that would never be sent. As the fourteen years became a time line, I noticed a clear pattern of abuse. It was like therapy to write out the words that I'd held hidden within me for so long.

When he tried to get me to engage in his nonsense, I felt no need to do so. I said my piece. He needed the turmoil to feel powerful, to affirm that he had power over me.

He tried and tried to get me back. He tried being nice, but I knew it was just a ploy. He tried being accusatory, but I told him I was free to do as I please, just like he had been. He tried to fight about the kids. You name it, he tried it. The problem was that I had seen with open eyes and an open heart that this man was never going to change. But I was ... I was taking my power back!

I want a happy life. I want love. I want a friend. It will never be him. He doesn't know how to love.

What he does know is that each time that he left, he taught me how to be more and more independent. He showed me how strong I really am. I know now that I was alone all along. His baggage of misery was blocking my doorway of happiness.

I feel free and happy. I'm remembering who I am. I am showing my boys how to treat a woman, self-respect and self-worth. They see the difference in me as well.

I loved the idea of this man. That man never really existed; that was the lure. The reality was much more grim.

I started listening to actions, not words. I am so grateful to now see the light.

I pray for his new prey.

I love me.

I love to paint ... I had forgotten.

I love to see nature and the beauty in everything ... I had forgotten.

—*D. Kyuss*

OUR LAST CONVERSATION

Dear G,

I tried talking about you again last night.

At one point, I referred to you as "that asshole," then promptly apologized: "Sorry, I'm working through a lot of anger this week."

My therapist shrugged, a half-smile dancing across his face. "You don't have to defend your ex-husband to me!"

It's not about defending you, this discomfort I have with the seductive nature of anger. It's not about defending myself either. Not like in the early months (or early years, if I'm honest), when I did not know how to hold you accountable without also unleashing a torrent of rage against myself: for my own failures, my own weakness, my compliance. I am more understanding towards myself now.

My mind was navigating land mines when I met you, and I learned over decades to tread around them with caution. I think they have all detonated now. While I still bear the wreckage, there is at last nothing left to diffuse.

Perhaps I should thank you for that.

I think I probably won't.

I.

AFTER WE SEPARATED AND I had a whole bed to myself, it took a full year before I relearned how not to sleep just on my side. My body arranged its curves to fit against your remembered shape, and I kept my left elbow pulled painfully behind my back. Do you remember how you trained me to sleep like this? How you would ask me to spoon against you, always the same accusing tone to your request ("Why don't you ever hold me? Why don't you ever want me to feel loved?")—yet when my arm lightly touched your body, or I rested my hand at your waist, you snarled with angry petulance: "I can't breathe! You're crushing me!"

It is hard to hold someone without using any of your limbs. It is even harder to convey love, under duress, to a body devoid of trust. Under your rigid stage direction, I suspect the best I managed to provide was warmth. And obedience, of course.

Still, I preferred this arrangement to our other common sleeping position: your leg wrapped around both of mine, your encircling arm holding both my own in a cross tight against my chest. Your body weight would pin me against the mattress as you rolled almost full on top of me, your front against my back.

"I can't sleep like that," I tried to explain. "I need to have some ability to move."

You explained, each time less patiently, how I was not, in fact, feeling trapped. This was how loving people slept. This was how loving people expressed their feelings.

Night after night, the same combat.

"Stop struggling," you hissed into my ear each time I tried to jockey enough space to let my ribs expand, and I would freeze at the angry tension in your voice.

Over time, I learned to will myself to sleep, to ignore the shallow breathing my squashed lungs could accommodate and to suppress the claustrophobic panic that threatened to climb up and out my throat. Each morning, we woke to find the fitted sheet corner by my head pulled completely off the mattress, as if desperate hands had sought to claw their way out.

"What do you do at night?" you'd laugh, as together we remade the bed.

Did you really not notice, before your own slumber, how far I tried to pull away from you? How I sometimes stretched a hand out to the floor, to brace myself against tumbling out of the bed altogether?

II.

I HAVE BEEN WORKING TO remember the good times between us, or even times that I thought were good when they were happening.

The way you claimed an early-evening bat had startled you, the first time you held my hand, and I knew the bat was both an excuse to grab for me—and something you found genuinely unnerving.

How you held me as I sobbed the morning my cat died suddenly, and I knew you'd stay with me as long as I needed, even though we were standing in the aisle of the church where you worked, and you had a choir waiting.

The first time you played me your favorite orchestral recording.

After our first date—that 2:00 p.m. meet-up for coffee that didn't end until 11:00, when the restaurant we had moved on to ended dinner service—I emailed a friend to say, "My expectations have forever been raised!" You had listened to me so intently, asked such interested and interesting questions about me, I could not imagine ever again settling for the standard first encounter, with tepid chitchat of "Where'd you grow up?" and "What do you do for a living?"

I used to include that date on my list of remembered good times, until I shared the story with a woman who herself spent years in therapy recovering from an abusive relationship. "Mm-hmm," she nodded at me knowingly. "Of course he listened carefully. He was studying you for weaknesses."

So our first date moved to the same list as our last, evidence to reference any time I plague myself with doubts.

Not that I need more than one item on that list. Whenever I remember our final date and picture the glee on your face at both my physical pain and my public humiliation—I am quite sure: things were rotten between us from the start. No one who had ever loved me could have treated me like that. No one who saw me as fully human would have even imagined it.

No memory is good enough to outweigh that ending.

—Alice Isak

CHANGING OF THE GUARD

I WOKE FROM A BAD dream this morning. My ex was trying to kill me. I was so glad to be awake. They don't come as often as they used to, which I am thankful for. The last time I saw him was 25 years ago. We were together for thirteen years before that. Not legally married, but a long-term relationship. Long enough to shatter my heart and soul.

My mother was what I would call a narcissist in many ways, which laid the groundwork for me to fall victim to yet an even stronger narcissistic personality in a man. It was familiar to me.

We met three months after my divorce was final. I had moved back in with my parents. I had a four-year-old daughter. I had quit school during my senior year, but had obtained my GED and was in a program to become an LPN. I was 22 years old. I had grown up in a dysfunctional family, so my confidence and self-esteem were low.

My mother and I did not get along, so I moved in with this person out of necessity. It was the biggest mistake of my life. I had no transportation of my own, so I was dependent on him from the beginning. I dropped out of nursing school because he said it took too much time away from our relationship. He said he would leave me if I didn't. Anytime I didn't come right home from a party or was out with my friends, he would say he would report me as abandoning my daughter.

It wasn't long before I started to notice behaviors. My family pictures would be laid face down. I wasn't allowed to see my family because he didn't like them. My best friend and I must be lesbians, because we talked on the phone often. Every minute had to be accounted for. I had no privacy. He would pick the lock when I was in the bathroom. He was verbally and physically abusive.

I eventually discovered all the lies. They are too numerous to mention. He was not divorced as he had told me, and he had two small children. He was not a graduate of ASU. He did not receive a purple heart while in Vietnam, because he was never in Vietnam. He said he knew brainwashing techniques from being associated with the CIA through the military. This I could almost believe because after so many years, I felt I might have been brainwashed.

He held himself in very high regard. He was intelligent, and could convince anyone of anything. He was very self-righteous and opinionated. He was quick to judge and condemn those who he felt were morally compromised. Right and wrong were absolute, with no gray areas. In his eyes my dad and brother were failures because they had made nothing of themselves according to his criteria. If I worked hard enough to "change" myself I might be able to overcome the failures of my family, but I would never get up to his level, but he was willing to accept that for my and my daughter's sake.

He would spend time helping my daughter with her schoolwork. This impressed me because to me it meant he cared about her welfare. He encouraged her to be the best she could be academically and otherwise. This stood out to me because my dad was quiet and distant emotionally. In reality this was just another ploy to gain our trust and tear us down at the same time. He had a son and daughter with his ex-wife. They were around the same age as my daughter. He resented my daughter and took it out on her when I wasn't around.

I would overhear him telling people I was mentally ill because I had depression in my family history. He would say I was a liar and not very smart. He suspected me of cheating on him all the time, although I never did. The last few years of our relationship I did get close emotionally to another man. I was scared to death he would find out. He had threatened my life in the past. He said he would track me down and kill me if he ever caught me cheating on him. He was especially fearful of me giving him AIDS. I thought it was a strange fear, because he knew I was devoted to him. I didn't know it, but he was doing to me what he accused me of doing.

He took business trips to the Philippines and Japan. He had girlfriends in both places. It was like he led several different lives. Although we were not legally married, he referred to me as his wife when it suited his purposes and had something to gain by it. We were engaged the first year we were together, but he kept pushing marriage further and further away as time went on. After years of this treatment I lost my identity. I didn't trust my own judgment because I was not allowed to use it in any situation. His word was always the final word.

Sometimes I would wonder why I didn't like someone or something, and it would be because he didn't like that someone or something. It was as if my own likes and dislikes were overridden by his. This happened with my mother as well. She would not let me wear the style of shoes I liked that were popular in grade school. It had to be what she liked. I had to have eyeglasses in the 6th grade. She picked out the frames and I hated them. She wanted me to be different, to stand out, but it had to be on her terms. All I wanted to do was be invisible, and not draw attention to myself.

My clothes and hairstyle had to meet with his approval. I had no choice over what was watched on television. If I was watching something he would simply turn it to what he wanted, without saying a word.

Any movie we would go out to see would be of his choosing only. Any vacation destinations or outings would be of his choice only. I couldn't refer to his friends as "our friends" because they were his friends only. I couldn't read any magazines he subscribed to if I didn't pay for half of the subscription. At Christmas, the tree was loaded with ornaments, tinsel, and angel hair. But none of it reflected me or my daughter.

My daughter wasn't allowed to receive cards or gifts from her father, because it meant there must be something going on behind his back between her father and me. Even as I type these words now I can't believe how I allowed this evil entity to control my life. Of course during this time he had me convinced there was something wrong with me, and I should be seeing a mental health professional. I did do that, and was told that if I got rid of him, any problems I was having would be solved. I should have listened.

During the course of these thirteen years I became an alcoholic. It seemed at the time it was the only thing that quieted my anxiety and panic attacks, but it just made them worse. I was caught in a cycle I couldn't seem to break out of. Even as I write this now all these years later my chest tightens.

My biggest regret is that my daughter was a victim too, and I kept her in that situation much longer than was necessary. It's bad enough for one person to have their spirit crushed. If only I would have been stronger. I can say that now, but at the time I didn't see it.

When she was nine years old she saw me writing on a sheet of paper over and over again the words, "I like myself." She asked me why I was writing that, but I couldn't tell her. I think I felt myself slipping away. It would take eight more years before I could emerge from the darkened, numbed state I was in.

Today there are many more resources and much more information available to those who are in this situation. Although it has been a long and arduous road, I feel I have found myself, buried below all the demands, wants, and needs of someone who was not worth one minute of it. I am still climbing up from that dark, deep hole of shame and isolation.

I want to be free.

—Starlene Schlim

I WILL SURVIVE

NINE YEARS TOGETHER.

I adored his arrogance; after all, he is gorgeous, he is brilliant, he is charming. He is talented, has a beautiful voice and could play guitar so well. He captured my heart and soul. I loved and worshipped him, and he loved me for it.

He was from the "OC." I was a hillbilly. I lived off-grid in the hills above a beautiful, small mountain town. I rode a quad, rode a horse, drove a four-wheel drive. I was a butcher at the local store, where we met. He was up north to install the solar system in a friend's cabin. Two weeks turned in to nine years.

He said I was like no other woman he had ever known and he was head over heels from the start. His friends from SoCal were completely surprised that this boot-wearing chick had captured his heart, but we were all convinced I had. We were the best of friends. I had no doubt when we married that it was for life.

On one of our many trips to Arizona, his mother's boyfriend showed us a house. It had an unbelievable view of the desert and the Colorado. It was big, with a three-car garage and a sprawling fenced yard with lots of room for animals. Immediately I thought of getting my mom to move out there with us. The deal was impossible to pass up. My mom came to visit in spring 2013 and was thinking about moving to live with us.

But then, life happened, as it does, and things came crashing down. My brother was murdered in July 2013. Of all the people I knew, I expected my husband to understand my pain, since he had been through the same heartache when his sister was killed. He didn't.

Four months later, on the worst day of my life, I went home to see my mom. I'd driven fourteen hours and when I finally arrived, Mom had passed away in her sleep. There was no warning. She went to bed and that was it. First I told my son and then I called my husband. Not once during the two months that it took to settle things did he come to be by my side. In fact, he spent that time gambling and drinking away his checks.

I expected him to support me, which was a mistake. In my sorrow, my focus was no longer on him, it was on surviving the devastation in my life. Every day of that year was mental warfare.

He left for two months in September 2014, three weeks after celebrating our 5th wedding anniversary at the place we got married.

The family property sold and made it through escrow in November. He came back the weekend I went to sign paper. Red flag, right? He was distracted, but things seemed fine. Then he got fired.

Suddenly the Tuesday and Wednesday evenings that we would spend at the local VFW playing pool changed. He got up and headed straight to the bar at 10:30 every Tuesday, then would go to the VFW for pool. We tended to argue when he drank early, so I quit going on Tuesday.

One day we were sitting at home watching a movie when he got a text from a girl he used to work with. One text said, "I'm in cabin 115 if you can get away." He said she was the stepmother of a friend and had made too much food, so she invited him over. My radar came on. In the midst of everything I had dealt with, I certainly did not want to think what I was thinking. He started drinking a lot more, often driving home drunk and rumors started about his behavior at bars. Several bartenders told me he was out of control. When I tried to talk to him about what was going on, he flew off the handle and said they were all lying.

Feeling like I may have been overly sensitive, I began investigating instead of accusing and fighting. I checked his cell logs and one number kept popping up all day on Tuesdays, starting at 10:30 a.m., until 8:00 or 9:00 p.m. when he would head to a casino and then not come home until 3:00 or 4:00 am. This went on for two months. The third time in a week he came home late, so drunk that he passed out on the bed in his shoes. I grabbed his phone. If I had been really smart, I would have read all the texts, but I just looked at his contacts. The Tuesday number belonged to the girl he used to work with. I woke him up. He said I was crazy, they were only friends, there was nothing going on, he loved me, he wouldn't do that. Then I said, "Give me your phone." He started yelling, packed his bags and went to his mom's house around the corner. I still live in "our" house.

For the next couple months, we would meet on Tuesday and Wednesday evenings when I got off work and met for dinner and drinks a couple of times. We talked on the phone and texted a lot. Got along and fought just like normal. We have been fiery from the start.

In May he asked me to help him sell some things (he never did computer work or paperwork) so I went to his email to see if anyone had responded to the ad I posted for his jeep. There weren't any replies to the ad, but an ex-girlfriend had sent him some nearly naked pictures of herself. Apparently they had been in contact for a while.

I turned off his cell phone, printed up divorce papers and sent him a video of our wedding pictures burning in the fire pit. He showed up. In typical form, I turned his cell back on. That Wednesday I had a heart attack. He was so concerned for me!

Over the next couple months we continued the same way until August when I threatened again to shut his cell off due to costly overages on the bill. He said he was working out of state and asked me to please leave it on for him to work. I agreed. Again. In September, he was over again. He swore it wasn't him using all the minutes, so I went to the call log and recited exactly whom he had been talking to and for how long. I turned his phone off. There has been no contact from him for a month but his new girlfriend texted me two weeks ago to let me know she had him now. I laughed and told her they were perfect for each other. Then I blocked her number.

Instead of being a good, loving, compassionate and supportive husband, he found another girl who worshipped him. I was destroyed. I could not believe he would do that, especially when I needed him so much. I had moved 1,000 miles from my hometown, all my friends, all my family, and my mom to be near his mother because she had had three heart attacks in two years. I never would have thought that the man I cherished could be so cold.

I first heard the word "narcissist" on a talk show. I could not believe my ears. My son was just as dumfounded by the perfect description of my husband. We searched the Internet and every story, every description, I saw was him in a nutshell. Everybody's words in the beginning came back to me. They all saw it, they all knew. They said he was as fake as they come, and that we would never work. He is back in Southern California now.

I was too caught up in his web to see what they saw then. I was too in love to see his many lies. Looking back now I wonder how I believed him and how I didn't see how very manipulated I was.

Now I understand. It is not his fault he has no empathy, even for the one he swore to love until death. It is just who he is.

He is a narcissist in every definition of the word. My friends tried to tell me, but I did not listen.

I lost time that I can't get back with family members that I will never see again. He took my confidence and strength.

He made me believe that I needed him. Then he showed me when I did need him, that I don't.

I will survive. I will thrive again. I am strong. I don't need him.

—Scarlet Fae

BEHIND THE MASK

I SLEEP AGAIN.

It happened suddenly and simultaneously as I walked into my new life.

My life is not yet clearly defined, but I have gained enough peace to be able to rest.

I have left behind the pills, the drugged nights and zombie days. My head is clear again, but my subconscious is hijacked by the trauma. The trauma, which has metamorphosed my life into something at once both familiar and unrecognizable.

I sleep deeply and think of the person who I loved, but never knew. I am me, as I always was, but you were never the person you pretended to be. I lay next to a stranger every single night. I lay next to something both unknowable and unworthy of the intense emotion and devotion I felt.

The truth of it threatens to overtake me at times, my mind in a relentless juxtaposition with my heart as my intellect informs my body that my lover DID NOT LOVE. All those moments that I cherished were simply nothing to you, an emotionless individual lacking any profound understanding of what I felt, and worse, lacking any care or concern for the legacy of damage your selfishness has placed in the core of my soul.

I loved an empty vessel, a shadow, a mimicry, a mask of nothingness. I lived in a house of cards that was built on a foundation of lies that you fed to me. My future was nothing more than a false bill of goods I had been sold by an actor.

I slept in that bed every night, my arms around your warm body, my toes twisted around your toes, your scent filling me with something that mimicked security, but you were always just lying in wait. You never bonded. You never held me and inhaled my scent with the beauty of knowing.

You never loved me.

A million times I have repeated this to myself and a million more I will still. You lie and scheme and fake and manipulate. You are still doing it now, to another poor soul who sees only what you want her to see. Until you can no longer control it, then she too will see behind the mask. It will slip and it will fall and the ugliness will still be there, the false self that you will never confront and never control. Because it controls you. You are a slave and it is your master.

I sleep again ... but the dreams escape me.

—Hope Jay

OLD DRESS, NEW SHOES

TODAY IS SUNDAY. LIKE ALWAYS, I get up early, get dressed, and drive to church; but today is different than every other Sunday of the last five years. It's rainy and dreary outside, a day when it would be so easy to sleep in and stay home and drown in my depression, but I don't. I'm actually looking forward to today. It may not seem like a big deal to some, but I'm wearing a new dress.

I saw it at the mall last night. I hadn't really wanted to go to the mall, but a friend asked me to go, and I knew that if I stayed home, I would just spend the night crying in bed, so I decided it would be better to stay busy.

I saw this dress at one of my favorite department stores, and thought, "That dress is really pretty—I don't have anything that color. Should I try it on? I really shouldn't spend the money. What does the price tag say? A $100 dress on sale for less than $50? Maybe I should see how it looks. Professional attire at a good price is never a bad idea."

I grabbed the size that I thought I would wear—the same size as the dress I purchased six months earlier—and went off to the dressing room. I was thinking that if it looked nice, I'd buy it; but if it didn't look so great, I'd save the money.

Could it be? The dress was too big! I'd been working on losing weight before the fallout happened, before I learned of my husband's affair, before he asked me to leave; but I'd plateaued over the summer when I couldn't focus on my diet and exercise because I was more focused on preserving my life, finding a new place to live, and visiting my lawyer's office.

I went to see if they had the next smaller size, never believing it would fit.

I really like this dress. It's a lovely combination of navy blue, turquoise, and purple. The top is a beautiful blend of paisleys that fades into a lovely print. The fabric is thin (like I like it, so I won't get too hot in the North Carolina humidity) and silky. Even though I think it's pretty on the hanger, I wondered... would it look okay on me? It's a nice dress, but would it look ugly with me in it?

That's what he would say. He hates paisleys and he hates dresses cut like this. He would say I look terrible in it.

I had an old dress before we were married that was similar to this dress. After the first few times I wore it in his presence, I stopped and only wore it on days that he didn't attend church with me, so he wouldn't have to be repulsed by looking at me in it.

At first, he told me that I owned better dresses, that this one certainly didn't flatter my body type. The next time, he grew a little more disgusted and said, "That is so ugly." Each time got a little worse, until I was told that wearing the dress was an act of disrespect to my husband.

Wearing clothes that he didn't like meant that I didn't care about him, even if I liked the clothes or even if I didn't have much to choose from. (I would always choose to spend money on his kids from a previous marriage instead of buying new clothes for myself.)

In his world, being married meant that my body belonged to him, so everything I did with my body was meant to please him, including the clothes I wore. I was property, and he believed that the Bible taught that the wife was the possession of her husband, not as a mutual submission, but as someone who existed for his pleasure and will. Not abiding by "the rules" of surrender to his demands meant that I suffered the consequences. I would get the cold shoulder in bed at night, the silent treatment during the day, and lectures on how disrespectful and childish I was when I begged him to talk about what was wrong in our marriage. He told me I was cold-hearted and that I didn't care about his opinions. I always ended up apologizing, promising to try harder and to be a better wife.

I kept the old dress hanging in my closet for occasions when he wouldn't have to look at me, simply because I liked it. It was colorful, modest, and stylish. It was a reminder of me. Who I was, or at least who I used to be.

One Sunday last year, he chose to stay home from church, so his nine-year-old daughter and I went alone. I wore the dress, and I'll never forget that day. It was just before he asked me to move out in May. His daughter said to me: "Miss Kerrie, you really shouldn't wear that dress."

"Why?" I asked. "This is a nice dress."

"Daddy does NOT like that dress. He has told you not to wear it. You should not wear clothes that Daddy does not like, you are supposed to dress in things he likes so he will love you."

That broke my heart. The little girl I was raising as my own was learning to find her value in what men thought of her clothes. The person wearing the clothes didn't matter at all ... it only mattered that the woman inside the clothes should lose herself and allow a man to tell her what she could and could not wear.

What was I teaching my stepdaughter by staying with this man? Was she learning that it was acceptable for women to be treated this way? That she should forget about what makes her comfortable, what she finds beautiful, what makes her independent, just to please a man? I didn't know who I was anymore.

I came from a good family, I had a master's degree, I had a good job, and I was successful; but I had let a man destroy me little by little, until I couldn't even wear a dress that I liked to church for a few hours. I wanted more for this precious little girl. She deserved to have a mind of her own, to be respected for who she is, and to decide what clothes she likes or doesn't like. She is beautiful inside and out, and heaven forbid a man tell her she is ugly in something that makes her feel attractive and comfortable with who she is inside.

It has been two months since I left; four months since he asked me to leave and since I discovered his affair. So there I was at the mall, conflicted over buying the new paisley dress. I didn't try on the smaller size, because I was sure it wouldn't fit, but I bought it anyway.

The next day, Sunday morning, I tried on the dress. It fit! It's a size smaller than I wore at Easter, and it's three sizes smaller than I wore this time last year—a non-scale victory to reward my hard work of diet and exercise.

I'm proud of myself, and I think it looks nice on me. I feel a small sense of victory over my abuser. Freedom. Freedom to be ME. I'm actually wearing a dress that I like, that was on sale, that is evidence of my weight loss, and that I know he would hate.

Yes, today is different. I don't have to worry about wearing a dress that may be considered "disrespectful" to my husband and his desires. I don't have to receive days of silent treatment for being insubordinate. I don't have to lay in a cold bed with a distant partner because my clothes are too modest and not sexy enough for him. I don't have to be berated and belittled for being myself.

Today, I saw a glimpse of ME again. I felt beautiful. I felt the liberty to be the woman God created me to be. I felt a release of anxiety knowing he could never hold me hostage in my own clothes again.

Although the best part is that I feel beautiful again, it is affirming to hear several people at church say, "I like that dress!" "You look nice today!" "That is so pretty!" I smile and say, "Thank you," and inside I pray that the young woman who said it will never know the pain of emotional abuse at the hands of a narcissist.

My new paisley dress is lovely. I am beautiful being the ME that God created me to be. The abuse is over for this moment. I can breathe, and I am free in my new dress.

Free to be me.

—*Kerrie Lee Clayton*

WHOLE AGAIN

The love you promised was a lie.

Hollow;

Like the tales you spin for your audience.

It's me?

It's the multiple mothers who came after our divorce.

It's your parents' fault.

It's society's fault.

It could never be you,

For you are the true victim;

The scapegoat who was falsely accused.

Arrested for no reason.

Serving prison time,

Several times over

Because the judges and police

Always take the woman's side.

Myself and how many others?

How many others will it take?

You never meant to hit any of us.

You just wanted us to be quiet.

You never meant to sleep with others.

While we were at home crying.

And cleaning up blood and broken glass.

You never meant to empty our bank accounts.

How sad for you

Your new friends say

You are so unlucky in love

Someday you will find a good woman

If only they knew the truth

How much would they adore you?

They are foolish
And believe your tales.
Those family members who know the truth
But live in denial—
They are all you will ever have
Ignorance to match your own.
I know the truth
And I have much more than you.
I have our children.
Beautiful, intelligent, happy.
Raised in a home with laughter and love.
No yelling and no violence.
No broken dishes.
No broken bones.
No blood to mop up.
Only happiness and safety.
Most importantly, peace—
Which all of your children
And their mothers deserve.
My nose, twice broken,
Can still smell the sweet scents of flowers
And holiday treats as they bake.
My fingers, gnarled and broken
On the hand you stabbed to the bone—
They can still write, and paint, and cook.
My arms that you bruised so badly—
They can still hug and provide comfort.
My jaw that you broke—
And the lips you often bloodied—
They can still laugh
And smile and sing.

The face you claimed was so ugly
Is once again beautiful.

Only this time I know it.

The body you claimed was so fat—

It is proud of the children it bore.

The mind you claimed was so stupid—

It is wiser than its years.

The heart you shattered—

It gives love

And receives love once again.

The scars both inside and out—

They give me character.

You can tell all the falsehoods you want.

You can place all the blame on those of us past.

But myself and the others,

We know the truth.

No matter what,

You could never break my spirit

The way that you broke my bones.

All of my pieces—

I swept them up

And put them back together.

I am whole again.

—Brandi Elizabeth

WHEN HELL CALLED

HE WALKED INTO OUR TWO-STORY colonial home a stranger, kissed me on the lips, and smacked my butt. I was fourteen. He was my stepfather and would continue to kiss and smack me well into my adulthood. I never liked it and was ignored for years when I asked that it stop. In order to keep the peace, I was forced to accept his insults, body shaming, and controlling, manipulative narcissism. I never liked him. Of course, in time, I grew to respect his money, and sometimes, the wounded child he was deep down. After all, he wasn't nearly as bad as my first stepfather, the one who, to this day, people still defend with love and authority.

The first stepfather was a violent monster who liked to stick his tongue in my mouth because "he just didn't know how to appropriately kiss little girls." I was five. He was a cop, a narcissist, and a drunk who liked to hit. He liked to hit a lot. Nowadays, selective amnesia is my family's preferred method of denial. I'm told it was all in my head, but the tired little girl who was dangled by her footie pajamas and threatened to be thrown down the basement steps for not cleaning up her Barbies remembers. In fact, the memory became a permanent scar, one which stretched across my search for future love and acceptance. I was molded and primed for relationships with narcissists since my early childhood and, as luck would have it, the worst was yet to come.

We met at a pub while I studied Irish Communal Identity and Travel Writing in Ireland. He was Irish, had electric blue eyes, and a very seductive accent. He seemed so exotic and I found that fascinating. My visa was about to end and I needed to head back to the states, but we vowed to keep in touch. It was during this time I was bit by the travel bug—hard. I had just graduated magnum cum laude from my university, had no formal job, no children, and nothing holding me back. So, I sold everything I owned and went on an adventure simply because I could. I traveled to five countries in two months before settling back in Ireland, where I reconnected with that mysterious fellow from the beer garden.

He wanted to "observe me in my natural habitat," so when my visa ran out again, he came to the United States to meet my family and friends and prove to me he was serious about our relationship. We talked about getting married and having children together. We had such a good time and I was so in love. He was such a romantic. We drank and laughed and made perfect love. It was a time of pure bliss. It didn't really bother me that he flipped out and became enraged when things didn't go his way because I understood he really needed a vacation. His job was very stressful because he was the only one who knew what he was doing. He was so confident and he reveled in his appearance. After my last failed relationship with a lazy frump, it was refreshing being with a man who took himself so seriously. He really seemed to be in charge and I liked that. Only in hindsight much later did I realize those behaviors were actually red flags that I didn't know I was ignoring.

Soon after he returned home, I found out I was pregnant. He called me all day while I was at the doctor. He didn't like it when he couldn't get a hold of me. He didn't like not knowing where I was at all times because he worried about me. When I told him our wish came true and that we were going to be parents, I wasn't expecting his initial reaction. Then again, it was life-changing news so I understood he was just scared. I was so excited as I packed my clothes and got ready to start our new life in Dublin. I couldn't wait to be the family of our dreams.

When I got off the plane he hugged me, put his hand on my growing belly and smiled. I was in heaven. We enjoyed a lovely dinner at a fancy restaurant and he brought me flowers whenever he got paid. But as I unpacked more of my things, his behavior toward me started to change. He became very critical and I could never do anything right. The dinners stopped, the flowers stopped, and shortly thereafter, the laughter stopped.

The pregnancy was beginning to show and no matter how hard I tried, no one would hire me. He controlled everything and afforded me nothing, because I was nothing more than a "gold digger." The doctor, who he picked, was an hour away and he would give me just enough money to cover the bus fare. I often traveled with no food, no snacks, and no water.

He refused to either buy me maternity clothes or spend a single cent on preparations for the baby. He made meals that he knew I couldn't tolerate or stand the smell of, but if I didn't eat it, I would go hungry. I never knew when he was going to go to the grocery store again. The same was true for cleaning products—though I was still expected to use them to clean. He often came home drunk after I would go an entire day without eating and still refuse to take me grocery shopping. I begged him to buy me toilet paper because, well, pregnant women pee—a lot. He threw a roll of paper towels at me and told me I better make them last. The emotional warfare was never ending.

There was hell to pay if I made toast and left crumbs in the butter. I had to endure the humiliation of a dishwashing lesson so he could be sure I was washing them to his satisfaction. He supervised me for a time to make sure I did it his way. He forbade me to speak during televised soccer matches when his favorite team played; that included sneezing. He often yelled at me because I spoke so loud that it hurt his ears. He couldn't stand the "stupid things" I said in my "dumb Yankee accent." When I recycled an empty glass jar that had been sitting on the counter for months without his permission, I was berated like I had just jumped in the car and ran over the family dog. As it turned out, I was the family dog and he only got us a car so that I could chauffeur him around because he never learned how to drive. He also informed me that his mother was to be my son's primary caregiver, because I was already dubbed an "inept mother." He was so arrogant and so entitled and I hated him.

He needed a break, so despite not having any money and the fact that I didn't want to go, he booked us a trip to Spain to see his older brother. The trip was a disaster the second I opened my "ignorant American mouth" and embarrassed him. When we returned, the Internet and phone were promptly disconnected. There I was in a foreign country, pregnant, with no food, no real medical care, and no way to communicate with the outside world, let alone my friends and family. I was absolutely terrified and this only encouraged him. He loved when I cried. He got off on it. At the sight of a single one of my tears, his brow would furrow and a smile would overcome his face to rival that of a vampire smiling and licking his lips at the sight of blood.

We started sleeping in separate bedrooms and I locked the door at night so I would feel safe enough to shut my eyes, even if it was only for an hour or two. I was exhausted, but I rubbed my tummy and hummed to my son to assure him I was going to figure out a way to get us far away from there. During particularly loud screaming matches, the baby would often stop moving and stay very still. When it was over, I would sneak off and talk to him.

"Are you okay in there? Mommy loves you very much, Peanut. Don't give up on me. I'm going to get us out of here. Just trust me and be patient," I told him as I tapped on my stomach and like magic, he tapped me back from the inside. Even before he was born we had an indestructible bond and I was determined to give him the life he deserved.

On one rather unremarkable day we were arguing at the top of the steps and he squared off on me. I was absolutely convinced that he was going to push me down the steps.

"This is it," I thought to myself. He is going to kill me. With every ounce of courage I had left, I walked toward him and pushed past him to a safer position away from the steps. I called my mother the next day to tell her I needed to get out. My son and I were no longer safe and his behavior was escalating out of control. Shortly upon her arrival, he took the key out of my door reminding me it was his house and insisted he would not have locked doors. The very next day while he was at work, I escaped and my mother flew us home.

At my first prenatal appointment stateside, I was handed a piece of paper to fill out. I just stared at the line where it asked for the father's name. He had previously informed me that I did not have his permission to put his name on anything since I was a whore and the baby probably wasn't even his. I was shaking and lost it. The hospital intervened and I was assigned a crisis counselor.

Through intensive therapy, I came to understand that something called "narcissistic personality disorder" was a real thing and that I was wise to leave when I did, as it was only a matter of time before he began physically assaulting me. At six months pregnant, I was diagnosed with PTSD and continued to work through my anger, fear and sadness. But, I always felt judged by my family, like I had it coming to me. Later, I was informed I was probably making it all up and besides "it's not like he ever hit me." Why couldn't I just get over it? I just liked playing the victim.

How did I let this happen? I was a well-educated feminist for Pete's sake! How did I not see this coming? I felt very sorry for myself and then something miraculous happened. Without prompting, I felt a little tap, tap from the inside. Despite my feelings of profound isolation, that very second, I dried my tears and focused all of my energy and resolve on breaking the cycle of abuse for my son. I vowed he would never suffer through fear at the hand of a parent and, to this day, I have kept that promise.

What we endured, the torment, the terror, the trauma, was finally a distant nightmare. We made it through. We were not broken. Instead, at long last, we were free.

—*Jessica Ayres*

LOVE-BOMBED

He wouldn't give it a rest,
I couldn't catch my breath.
If given the chance, he would
Have love-bombed me to death.
He wanted to be the
Foremost thought in my head;
The first when I awoke
And the last one before bed;
He wanted me to want him,
To be my obsession,
All so he could claim me
As another prize possession.

I have to face facts—I
Was targeted and groomed.
Only to be dropped
After I had been consumed.
I stopped playing along,
Didn't fall into his plans;
Slipped through his grasping fingers
Like tiny grains of sand.
I didn't escape unscathed,
My heart forever fractured,
The pain and sorrow I feel
The only emotions not manufactured.

—Autumn Ray

THE CONFAB

I'M NOT A THERAPIST. I didn't even minor in psychology. I'm just a woman who fell head over heels in love with a man, married him, then pretty quickly (or too slowly, depending on your sense of time) realized that he was not who he seemed to be. My world crumbled, and this is my attempt to pick up the pieces and make sense of it all.

I'm still having a hard time believing that all I learned was real life. Nothing he said was true. What I thought was real, was not real. What I thought my life was, was not my life. I trusted him. I believed him. Everything I believed was a lie.

I wonder now if anything was real. Did he love me even a little? Or is he not even capable of love? Did he ever feel anything for me? I always got the sense that what I felt for him was unrequited, but maybe he honestly never even cared about me, not even a little.

I did so much for him. He did nothing for me. In a way, I suppose, why would he? He never loved me. He never cared. It wasn't real. It was all fake.

It's a lot to process, and I'm not really processing it, if I'm being honest. I'm numb. I'm not sad or angry. I feel nothing. It's too much cognitive dissonance. I simply can't wrap my brain around it.

He had another relationship going while he was married to me.

He fathered another child.

He was living another life.

Everything was a lie.

What's been at least a little bit comforting was learning that he treated his ex the exact same way, as I discovered by emailing her. He has a son with a previous girlfriend. They broke up in 2010, and the last time he saw his son was 2012.

At first I believed him when he said that she was a horrible person, but as time went on and I learned who he really was, I began to feel nothing but sympathy for her. He left her when she was seven months pregnant. He chose his career over her and his son, just like he did to me. I knew that she and I had a lot in common, and I always wondered about her.

She wrote back a lovely email to the message that I'd sent. She was shocked to hear from me, but also happy. She said that she felt guilty for not warning me, but knew that I was just as taken with him at the beginning as she had been, and knew that I wouldn't have listened anyway (totally true).

She confirmed that their pattern was exactly the same as his and mine—at first it was blissful and perfect, then he began to change, and then suddenly she realized that she was stuck in a terrible relationship and pregnant.

He was also angry and violent with her. He told her outright, just like he told me, that he would always choose his career over her. She paid for everything for him, just like I did. He also criticized her physically, and made her believe that she was much less than him. It took her years to realize that it was the other way around, and that SHE was the strong, talented one, and he was a sick, sad man.

She's now married to a "wonderful, caring man," and in addition to the son with my husband, her husband has three children, and she gave birth to a baby girl earlier this year. She is happy. She promised me that I would be one day as well, and that I am too smart and too good to let him ruin me. She gave me hope.

I know it wasn't me. The problem wasn't me, it wasn't her, it wasn't his current (or now recent-ex) girlfriend. It's him. He is the sick one. He is the one who hates himself, and who is damaged beyond repair. We don't have to be.

We have the capability to love and trust, which is what you are supposed to do when you're in love. People who love you aren't supposed to lie and cheat and deceive.

He's the one whose life is all a charade. Mine life is real. My feelings were real. I behaved in a way that was truthful and in a way that you'd expect when a person loves another person. He did not. My life will continue. His never began.

—*Erin McGee*

THE HIROSHIMA OF BOMBSHELLS

THE OTHER WOMAN CALLED ME today. I emailed her an apology yesterday for a nasty email I'd sent her in anger when I first found out about the affair. The more I thought about it, the more I realized that I had been extremely unfair to her, and that my anger needed to be squarely directed at my husband, not at her. So I apologized and gave her my Skype name, should she ever want to talk in the future. Five minutes after hitting "send," she tried calling me.

She called me a few times, and though I answered each time, she kept hanging up. Then she signed off. I thought maybe she got cold feet, which is understandable, so I sent her a message letting her know that I'm open to talk any time that worked for her.

Today, she called. I answered. And we spoke for over an hour.

The hang-ups, I learned, were because my husband was there in the room with her, batting the phone out of her hand and trying to break it as she called me. So she waited until he left today to call.

They met in January, and the affair began right away. He's been living with her all year. Each time he left me, he moved in with her. She showed me his suitcases and his PS4 (that I bought him). She's close with his parents, and talks to them almost every day.

"I want to tell you everything, but I don't want you to be hurt any more than you already are. I respect you as a woman, and I don't want to hurt you," she said.

"I promise you that there is not much that would surprise me at this point. I've already lost everything, and I don't really think I can be hurt any more at this point."

"You have no idea how much I have lost. You can't imagine."

"I can, and I'm sure that he is also bleeding you dry, just like he did me. And I know that you have even more to lose financially than I did."

"It's so much more than that. I want to tell you, but I don't want to hurt you, and I don't want you to tell him."

"I promise I won't tell him. I never want to speak with him again. Can you please tell me?"

"I was pregnant. He wanted me to keep it. But I didn't want to. I didn't want that life."

Somehow, even though this was new information, I knew this in my gut. I nodded and said, "I know." And I then began to cry. "I'm so sorry for you. I'm so sorry that you had to go through that."

"So that was why he left me one day in March, then? That's why you were in the hospital?" I continued.

"Yes. His parents called to let him know I was dying. I also tried to kill myself two times after that."

I cried again. "I'm so sorry. I'm so, so sorry. I almost killed myself too, last fall. He almost killed both of us."

She nodded.

"All I have now is my money. I have nothing else. My life is shattered," she said.

"I understand. I never had money, but he took all of it."

"I know," she said. "I told myself that he must have no money because he was sending you all of it, so I paid for everything for him."

"I knew that you paid for everything. I found the receipts for the flights. You even paid his way back to me. That was extremely kind of you."

"I paid for everything."

"I know he spent his money on child support and taxes—"

"He didn't pay any of that. I paid all of that. Because I thought he was spending all of his money on you."

I laughed. "Sweetheart, in the three years we were together, he paid for nothing. NOTHING. Not one bill. I paid for everything. We were both paying for him."

We talked about many things, most of which are a blur. But she really did seem to know all about everything. He told her as much, if not more, about his life than I knew. She knew about his exes, how he was also abusive to them. She was a victim in this just as much as I am.

"I can't imagine how you must be feeling. I promise you, I am not with him, and I will not be with him. I don't want him in my life. I want him gone. He's coming by to get his things later," she assured me.

"I don't want him either. Don't be alone. He can be so violent when he's angry. And right now, his entire web of lies has exploded on him. He must be short-circuiting. I can't imagine how angry he is. Be very careful."

"I know." She nodded.

"Call me or text me when he's gone to let me know that you're okay. I'm worried about you."

We thanked each other, and we apologized to each other again. We empathized; even though we were on opposite sides of the issue, we'd both been destroyed by the same force. She sent me love and hugs and kisses, and I sent the same back to her. She said to call any time I needed anything, and I told her to do the same.

He will not control us anymore.

—Erin McGee

THE WEEK BEFORE THANKSGIVING

IT WAS ONE WEEK BEFORE Thanksgiving when he broke up with me again. Of course, it was my fault. After several months, I'd grown tired of his ex-wives always changing plans with his children and in the process, changing my plans with my children, my friends, and with him. This happened often. Since he lived so far from me, we tried to keep the same visitation schedules with our children. This time I let him know that there were court papers and visitation guidelines for a reason and that he needed to utilize them. He broke up with me because I "just couldn't handle his life."

Our relationship had been on and off again for three years. But this time was different. I had already told him that it was now or never. I was tired of the games. If he didn't want to be divorced from his ex-wife, then by all means go back home to her, but leave me alone. Things got better, for a while.

He was a truck driver who was gone a lot, including many weekends. This particular week he came home on Friday. When he got home, he called me to tell me that his father had suffered a stroke the night before and they didn't know if he was going to make it. Then he began trying to get me to take him back. Again.

He spent the next couple of weeks messaging and calling. Always the same, "I love you so much. I miss you so much. I just can't live without you." I talked to him, but stood firm on not taking him back this time. I also informed him that I would be spending the majority of the Christmas season with my children and their father. I was already depressed and needed the positive influence.

One morning in early December, I arose to take my son to school. I made myself a cup of hot tea and sat down to check my social media while waiting for him to get ready. The first status that I saw was from my ex. It read: "Well, it's official. At 2:13 am this morning I killed three 17 year old kids in an accident."

He went on to describe how he had been in Iowa and had just gotten back on the road around 2:00 a.m. to make it to his first stop on time. He said that there had been an officer with someone pulled over, so he switched into the left lane. He said that as he checked his mirrors to make sure he had passed the other vehicles, a black Ford Ranger with three teenage boys crossed the grassy median, flew through the air and hit his truck.

Immediately I called him to check on him. He answered, telling me that he was waiting in the emergency room and had time to talk. He described further details of the accident. He cried as he told me that the boy that was driving died in his arms. It was such a horrific story. I cried for him. Not only was I worried for him, but my heart was so broken by this tragedy. My daughter was 17 and had just been in a mild accident weeks earlier. I couldn't imagine how these families were going to get through this. How was he ever going to get beyond this? I offered to take time off of work to drive out and get him. He turned me down, saying that someone from his company's safety department was coming and that they would rent him a car to drive home.

A day later, he sent me a picture of a boy who had been severed in half and had his left arm ripped off. "I did this," he said. I was mortified that he had this picture. I asked him how he got it. He said that since he was once in the safety department, they had accidentally forwarded all of the accident information to him, as well as the rest of the team. When I wasn't having nightmares about that picture, I still was unable to sleep as I thought about the nightmares he surely was having.

A few days later he called to let me know he was home and was on his way up. "I need to see you. I need to hold you," he said. I had a few hours before I had to go to work, so I agreed to see him. When he arrived at my apartment, he had a leg brace, wrist brace, neck brace and he shook uncontrollably. The tears seemed unstoppable. I wept from just seeing him. I was just so happy that he was alive!

He and I went to the park to talk for a couple of hours. It didn't go according to his plan, since I still refused to take him back. It didn't matter how much I loved him or how much I wanted to be with him, he always put everyone else before me and pretended that I didn't have needs. I knew that I didn't want to live like that.

I went to work that evening as usual. About three hours into my shift, I received a text message from his number, but it said it was his ex-wife. She demanded to know "Did you do this on purpose? Get him all the way up there to just completely destroy him like this?" I didn't know what to say. I didn't even know what was going on, except that this woman was accusing me of things that I knew nothing about.

Shaken, I showed the message to my coworker and we decided that I shouldn't respond to that message. A second message came through about twenty minutes later, stating, "This is your fault. I would never have encouraged him to come up and try to work things out with you if I had thought you would do this to him. I just don't think that it's right that he's back there having his stomach pumped because of you. He took a whole bottle of Lortab and drank a fifth of vodka. This is your fault."

I immediately left work, picked up my mother and drove an hour to get to the hospital. When we went in to find him, they informed us that he wasn't there. He hadn't been admitted to that hospital since 2008 (this was 2014). I called his phone, but didn't get an answer. Shortly after, his ex-wife messaged me. She told me he had gone to a different hospital where he had been admitted and that he would be moved to a psychiatric unit for evaluation.

Of course, a few days later, he was back. This time I was too shaken and weak. I was worried about him and I loved him. I agreed to take him back. He, my son, and I looked at houses and found a perfect home. We were to move in the beginning of February, which was only about three weeks away.

I agreed to marry him. We selected a date in July at a beautiful place in Tennessee, where we were going. I even had my dress picked out and was going to see a woman the following week about having it made.

In January, his employer was holding a safety banquet for their employees. He had been adamant about the time that we needed to leave my house. I rearranged my work schedule, working a double on Friday so that I could have Saturday off with him. When I got up from my nap to start getting ready, I hadn't heard from him yet. That was strange because he always kept in touch with me. I texted and called multiple times, to no avail.

About a half an hour after we should have left, he finally returned my call. He had told me earlier in the week that his youngest son had run away from school and from his aunt's house where he and his mother were living. He said that the boy had been diagnosed as slightly autistic. He explained that because of his anger and running, they were taking him to a mental health facility for help.

Sometimes, it isn't just our hearts that break. Sometimes it's something in our head, too. I felt the break that day. I felt that I was living where multiple personalities were made. I became two people inside my head. I couldn't tell you how many hours I sat in the window, in a state of complete disconnect from the rest of the world, just trying to understand.

Two days later, I spoke to his wife. No, she wasn't his ex. She had never cheated, they had never filed for divorce, their son had never run away and while he was ADHD, he was not autistic.

There had never been an accident involving teenagers, nor had there been a suicide attempt. I also discovered that when he had brought his oldest son (by an actual ex-wife) to meet me and my son, he had threatened the boy that he better not tell anyone or he would sell all of his belongings.

I spent several weeks in a state of deep depression, lying on the couch crying. My otherwise stellar work ethic fell by the wayside. So did my hygiene. Thank God for my best friend that gave me options. It was either shower and shave my armpits, OR she was doing it for me. It was motivational and it worked.

I felt that because she was his wife, my feelings were invalid. That not only was I his whore, but also a home-wrecker as well. I felt so guilty and ashamed of myself and my behavior. It didn't seem to matter that I didn't know he was still married or that I believed he and I were building a life together. I lost 20 pounds because I couldn't eat. I didn't sleep. My anxiety reached new heights. I became paranoid of my surroundings, and I began having suicidal thoughts.

I wanted to get better. I hated feeling this way and hated him even more for making me feel this way. That's when I discovered narcissism. He was a textbook case.

At this point, while not frequently, he was still contacting me. One message during this time read, "I was going to kill myself last night, but forgot the bullets." He sent that to me on my birthday while I was out of town. (He had threatened suicide dozens of times already.)

Less than a month later, after a visit to my doctor, I filed a no-contact order against him. Coincidentally, a week after it was filed, someone called my boss to inform him that I was on drugs. It was one of many untrue stories he told about me.

Soon, it will be a year and I still struggle regularly. I fear he will always be a shadow over my heart. I'm thankful for God, my friends, and my family who have stood with me and seen me through this. I couldn't have done it without them.

I know now that it was my strength of character, empathy and compassion that attracted him to me. I also know that I will not change who I am because of him.

I know that he is the one that is broken, not me.

I know that I AM A SURVIVOR.

—Missy Jones

REALIZING I'M NOT ALONE

MEETING MY FUTURE HUSBAND WAS a dream come true. After being teased all of my childhood, someone finally loved me for who I was. I knew I would have a problem-free marriage. After all, I was going to marry a pastor. My marriage was going to be the turning point in my life.

Well, it was the turning point. Just not quite the kind that I'd imagined it would be ...

Communication was always an issue when we were dating. If I tried to talk about something, he would change the subject or suggest that we go to a movie. I assumed he was slow to warm up—shy and quiet. I was wrong.

He never did begin to talk about any issues or any decisions in our marriage. I tried to discuss how we were going to discipline our children. At first he would say, "We'll cross that bridge when we get to it." Later, he would push off the conversations by going to a movie, golfing, or calling someone. Our kids are almost grown and we never did "cross that bridge" of how to discipline them.

I can't pinpoint an exact time frame when I realized things were wrong. The issues just seemed to sneak up on me over time. One day, I was a capable wife and the next I heard the person who was supposed to love me more than anyone calling me a "terrible excuse for a wife." The next day, all seemed to be fine again. Maybe I'd just imagined what he had said.

I wish I could say it was all my imagination, but the harsh words continued and got worse. I always had an excellent memory, so when he started telling me, "You never told me about ..." or "I never said that," I wondered if I was losing my mind.

I felt like I was going crazy from the confusion. At times, he would even say the exact opposite of what I had told him. I began to feel like I was living with an Alzheimer's patient because I could tell him something one minute and he would deny that I had told him that just minutes later.

Was it me or was it him? My mind would go round and round in circles. I would tell myself, "I know I told him ..." but then I'd doubt, "Maybe you just thought you told him ..." I lived in a state of constant confusion.

Knowing we needed help, I turned to a counselor. Notice, I said I turned to a counselor; he didn't think we had any problems and was not about to see a counselor. Over the years, I went to a few different counselors. He would come for obligatory appointments as requested by the counselor. He would nod politely when spoken to. Then, on the drive home, he would insult me and yell at me. I was left wondering if he had even heard anything the counselor said.

There were times I was thinking clearly and I was positive something wasn't right about him, but I never found any proof until one morning when he was leaving for a meeting. He made sure to tell me over and over that I needed to pick up our child from school.

He drilled that into my head because "I'll be at the meeting and I won't be able to leave, so you need to remember. You won't forget." No, I would not forget. After I picked up our child, we happened to see another person who had been at this meeting. He commented that they had missed my husband at the meeting. Shocked, I answered, "He wasn't there? He said he was going." By the look on this other person's face I could tell he realized something wasn't right. He quickly stated, "Well, maybe something came up," but the look on his face revealed that he didn't believe what he had just said.

Time progressed slowly and painfully for me. I grew to dread the sound of the garage door indicating he had arrived home. My body would tense up in anticipation of his unhappiness. If I had played with our kids that day, he would bark, "God, why can't you ever clean up this mess! It looks like a pig sty!" So, the next time, I decided I'd clean and let the kids entertain themselves. I thought he would be happy. I plopped down on the couch, exhausted, around the time the garage door went up. Instead of a compliment, he said, "Is that all you do all day, sit on your lazy butt and ignore the kids?" I was never sure what to do and it didn't matter anyway because he would not be satisfied.

For the last four years of our marriage, he accused me of having an affair with someone. He knew I wasn't having an affair (I barely left the house because he was gone at every meeting and activity he could find to participate in so he would not have to be home with us), but he still accused me of it. I confronted him many times about this accusation, but it made no difference to him. He might stop saying something for a few days, but then he would start referring to my "boyfriend" in front of the kids.

Not only did he accuse me of having an affair, he was so crafty and conniving that he was putting the ideas in my mind that this other man was in love with me and would leave his wife so we could be married and have a Disney "happily ever after" life. My mind was caught between the reality of knowing I was not having an affair versus the slick talk that sounded so true, so convincing, so real, and so promising. Was I going insane? Why would my husband say such things? Was it true?

My mind raced constantly. My shoulders ached day and night. I feared I was going crazy. During this time, I was fortunate to have a very good counselor who was able to recognize this as emotional abuse. It was during this phase that I filed for divorce, completely confident that I would get custody of our kids.

We didn't have much money, so we decided to hire one lawyer. We didn't know that one lawyer can't represent both of you, so, legally, I hired the lawyer. I wasn't impressed with him, considering every few words from his mouth were some type of swear word. When I told him about the things my husband had said and how he treated me, the lawyer claimed he talked to his wife like that all the time and he stated, "What did you do to deserve it?" I wondered whose side this guy was on. Even though I was about as low as a person could be emotionally, I knew I was getting enough of that attitude from my husband and I did not need any more of it. I had no choice but to go without a lawyer.

My husband used my situation to take further advantage of me during the divorce. He knew me well enough to find my weak spots and he used them. "When you're sick in bed with a migraine, how will you take care of the kids?" "What will you do with the kids when they don't have school and you have to work?" As the days went on, he ratcheted up the harassment to the point of threatening to expose my "affair" if I did not sign the decree. I cried. I pleaded. I begged. He pressured all the more. How did he get me to sign? It was the night before the funerals of both my grandmother and a friend of mine. He took advantage of my emotional state and told me he was "getting the worse end of the deal." By getting full custody of the kids?

Emotionally, I could go no lower. Because of my childhood, I never had much self-esteem. Any shred of who I was disappeared. My goals in life—to be married and to be a mom—were both ripped away from me with one signature. Because the home went with his job, I did not have a place to live. I had no money. My insurance was through his job, and that was gone, too. He had promised me he would help pay my rent and would give me back the items that belonged to me from our house. He paid less than half of my rent for one month. I waited close to three years and I never did get most of my items back, some of which I'd had since childhood.

My life was bleak then. I wish I could say that the divorce made him change, but it didn't. He continues to make bad choices. Following our divorce, he married and divorced quickly. Now he is preparing to get married for the third time. As a result of his behavior, he lost his job, insurance, home. He and our kids have lived in three different houses within a month. Still, he blames me and others. He takes no responsibility for what has happened.

Slowly, oh so slowly, in much the same way that the abuse came upon me, I have begun to learn about these kinds of people. First, it was through a local center for victims of abuse and assault. When I got insurance, I returned to the same counselor I had been seeing prior to the divorce.

I cried and cried as I sat in her office. I was angry. I was frustrated. I was upset. I lamented, "Why did the person who caused all these problems get custody? Why is he allowed to be with my kids all the time and influence them when I can't? Was getting divorced the wrong thing to do? Should I have stayed married? Did I make a mistake?"

I will never forget her answer because it was the most eye-opening thing I have ever heard. My counselor told me, "If you hadn't gotten divorced, I wouldn't be talking to you right now." She paused for a moment while I thought, "Yeah, I'd probably be talking to some other counselor?" Then, she continued, "You would be in a mental institute or you would have killed yourself from the stress."

No, I'll never be the same. How can you be after the person who promised to love you forever betrays you and hurts you so badly? With the help of counselors, articles, websites and online support groups, I have discovered the names for everything that I have experienced: gaslighting, crazy-making, projection, etc. I have a word to describe my ex: narcissism.

And, I am realizing I am not alone.

Neither are you.

—*Kelly Meadows*

I'M BACK

EIGHT YEARS AGO I LOST myself in religious fundamentalism. I wasn't raised that way; my family was what I would call "secular by default" with no particular religious leaning.

By the time I was in college, I considered myself an atheist and liberal in my political beliefs. I participated in normal college activities, went to a ton of concerts and marched in protests.

Then I had a rough breakup, most of my friends graduated, and I moved off campus and was more distant from other friends and family. I was lonely. I started going to church with a college acquaintance. The church was not strict fundamentalist, but still pretty conservative.

This is really where the changes started.

The thing you have to realize is that you can't look into fundamentalism with your outside rationalism. The most important aspect of fundamentalism is pleasing God. He is the ultimate authority figure. Nearly anything is permissible under the guise of this belief, including atrocities.

I was always a Goody Two-shoes. I was the high school valedictorian and graduated magna cum laude from college, from where I was accepted into vet school. I was a go-getter and didn't want to displease the authority figures in my life. So if there was no greater authority than God, of course I wanted to please him. I've never done anything halfway, so I was all in.

Then I met my narcissist, a fundamentalist. This is where things got dangerous. When I was attending the first church, some of my opinions changed and even some of my friends, but I was still going to concerts, drinking alcohol and my attire remained the same.

When I met him I jumped off the deep end with him. Here's why: he wasn't just a "guy" and it wasn't just about "love." In fundamentalism your husband is not just the man you love, he's your authority figure, too. Displeasing him displeases God. So there's this double authority over women. Disagreeing over what color to paint the living room isn't just an argument with your spouse, it's displeasing the creator of the universe. If you wonder why women in these churches don't leave, that's why. It's a serious guilt trip.

Initially our relationship was good. I wanted to please God and loved this man that I wanted to please. Conveniently enough, by pleasing him I pleased God.

We got married and had a baby. At this point I was almost unrecognizable from the person I'd been just three years prior. I wore skirts exclusively. I didn't listen to any secular music, watch TV or go to the movies. I didn't drink alcohol or associate with anyone that did. My political beliefs completely reversed. I was the polar opposite of who I had been before.

After my son was born, I saw a tiny crack in my husband's personality. Our son was born at home with a midwife. I was an ardent home-birth supporter at the time. Afterward I found out that she and my husband had conversations during the labor that I wasn't privy to—life or death decisions that I didn't get a say in.

I started researching home birth and completely changed my mind. By 2012, I no longer supported home birth. And then he found out.

We had one argument over the topic. He called me "Miss Independent" and a "feminazi," the worst insults he could think of when the wife is supposed to be submissive to her husband. The argument ended with him deciding that the only way to resolve the disagreement was to not get pregnant and the only way to guarantee I wouldn't get pregnant was to be abstinent.

I should have left at that point, but I was in deep. Divorce is really never an option in fundamentalist churches and I honestly never even thought about it. In fundamentalism, if there's a problem you are always to blame. The solution is always for you to try harder. So that's what I did.

I tried even harder to be the good Christian wife. We moved, joined a new church and actually met a couple folks in the church that he considered holy enough for us to be friends with. Things got better for a time. We had another baby. It was a planned home birth, over my silent objections, but I wanted to preserve the harmony of our marriage.

There were complications and we ended up transferring to the hospital. Thankfully everything was okay, but that sealed it for me. I couldn't get by being silent and internally disagreeing with him.

Nine months later I got pregnant again. This time I put my foot down and demanded a hospital birth, so he refused to be a part of the pregnancy. He said he wouldn't come to the birth and wouldn't bring our son to see me in the hospital. I went to my first appointment alone. When I had some bleeding at eleven weeks, I went to the office alone to find out if my baby was still alive. It was. When the bleeding returned, I was alone when they couldn't find the baby's heartbeat. I went to the hospital alone for an emergency D&C.

That summer was a very lonely time. I'd lost "my" baby. (It wasn't "our" baby. It was "mine.") He was furious with me. He blamed me for the miscarriage, saying it was God's punishment for not submitting to him. Ultimately that's what it was about. Not the topic of home birth particularly, but that I dared have an opinion different from his and refused to change for him.

We had another argument about home birth versus hospital birth. He looked right at me and said, "You know, sometimes I seriously wish you were just barefoot and ignorant in the kitchen." In that moment I decided to leave. It was a very fast and clear decision. He didn't want me. Everything I'd done was never going to be enough. I was an intelligent, thinking person and he didn't want that.

Twelve days later I moved out and filed for divorce. It took several weeks to completely break free from him. At a doctor's appointment, I saw a poster of the Duluth Power and Control Wheel. That's when I realized that what I'd experienced was verbal and emotional abuse.

My therapist recommended that I read a book, *The Verbally Abusive Relationship*. In that book, the author addressed narcissistic personality disorder (NPD). After some time researching NPD I found that the most telling trait is a lack of empathy. Much like the decision to move out and the recognition of my marriage as abusive, this was another "lightbulb" moment. Shortly after I miscarried "my" baby, I was crying as he stood there, unbelieving that I was upset he hadn't been with me at the hospital. I had told him, "You have the empathy of a rock." He turned and walked out. I didn't know it at the time, but I had diagnosed his narcissistic personality disorder.

The revelations that my marriage had been abusive and that he was a narcissist really set me free. There wasn't something wrong with me, which is what he and the church had said; how he treated me was wrong. I had to get as far from him and that life as I could and back to who I was before, back to who I really was inside.

Life after him has been so incredibly exciting and fun and liberating. I've shopped for a new wardrobe. I've gotten drunk. I've rediscovered all my old favorite bands. I've reconnected with friends. More importantly, I've reconnected with my parents and they're getting to enjoy their only grandbabies for the first time.

I'm still not sure where my "self" is going to settle. My life had swung so far to one side of the pendulum that I'm sure in some ways I'm far out to the other side right now. Take miniskirts for example—I never would have worn one before I met him. I just wasn't comfortable in short skirts and preferred long skirts. But after years of mandated long frumpy skirts, I just can't bring myself to wear them. So we'll see.

I've been out a little more than a year now. I recently attended my first Dave Matthews Band concert in nine years. I LOVE the Dave Matthews Band and had been to 15 or 20 shows before I met him, so getting back to a concert was hugely important to me. As I danced and sang and listened to that music I kept thinking, "I'm back." I'm back at a show and I'm back.

I was gone for a while. But I'm back now.

—Ashley Dunn, DVM

CHAPTER 2

COURAGE AND WORDS
OF ENCOURAGEMENT

*One of the most courageous decisions you'll ever make is to finally let
go of what is hurting your heart and soul.*
—Brigitte Nicole

WARTIME

SOMETHING I REALIZED TODAY: IT'S always wartime in a relationship with a Cluster B Narcissist. Remember this. Every single move they make, every word out of their mouth, every fiber of their being is to get one over on their "opponent." This is how their mind works. They are the reigning superior who needs a "combatant."

We may think of ourselves as victims. They may place us in a victim role. But really, we are warriors carefully selected, not for our weaknesses (e.g., insecurity, perceived inferiority, low self-esteem), but for their counterstrengths (i.e., vulnerability, compassion, empathy, kindness, monumental capacity for love).

The narc's game is to take us down by siphoning our spirit. While we believe that we are in the playful game of love, courtship, relating, friendship, or family, we are actually in a constant state of spiritual combat with a soulless demon. Remember this especially when they come back with the nice voice, the favors, the snuggles, the benevolent gestures, and the "gifts." These "peace offerings" are cleverly designed to lull us into our humble grace of believing that everyone has good in them. Yes, everyone does have good in them. But not everyone uses their power of good for the ultimate purpose of goodness. The narc uses every tool in their wheelhouse for one purpose only: to take down their opponent. Always. As long as we remain engageable as a combatant, they will get a piece of us.

Once we are able to relate with our own self from a place of self-empowerment and strength, we become imperturbable and immune to their crafty ways. This is when they drop us. And please believe me, being dropped by them is the best scenario possible. I know it hurts. I know it's messy. But it is far better than the alternative of living as only part human with a crushed spirit, or worse, no life at all.

Never tell them you are in a state of weakness; they love to kick us when we're down. Never tell them what you love; they adore taking it away from us and keeping it from us. Never confide in them; they will always use it against us. Never let them know what makes you happy; they live to interfere with the happiness of others. They will go miles out of their way for these "adventurous battles." You can spend your entire lifetime trying to figure out why, but there is no reason why. The sooner you learn this, the better.

For those of you who are still young, please know this and do not spend any more of your precious and glorious life trying to figure out why they do what they do, what's wrong with you, or what you can do to "help" them. In the end, it will not matter. All you will learn is that the only reason they did those things was to waste your lifetime focusing on them. That is their ultimate win. They are not called "please help me, I am troubled." They are not called "I just haven't met the right person who understands me." They are not called "I must be saved." They are called "narcissist: look at me and only me forever and ever."

My famous examples:

My mother: "At least I never hit you."

My ex-abuser: "The scary thing about you is that you're smart."

My ex-fiancé: "I want to trap you so you can't get away from me."

My ex-best friend: After telling me she made out with the guy I liked, "He was a bad kisser."

I am fifty-one now, and after nearly a lifetime of trying to figure it all out, I have learned the above in the last brief four months of researching information such as that provided by the kind folks in this forum and people like Bree Bonchay, LCSW, Bobbi Parish, M.A., and Athena Moberg, CPC. I have been told that my information inspires and helps others. I will not say that going through what I survived was worth being able to help others. But if I can help others with what I have learned, that helps me recover what I feel I have lost to this ridiculous farce of a circus that was my life as a gullible lover of humanity.

—*Dawn Stott*

BREAK THE CYCLE

A FRIEND OF MINE RECENTLY opened up to me about her current relationship with an abusive narcissist, knowing of my previous experiences. She asked, "When does it get better?"

"When you finally get away," I replied.

She was in a state of disbelief, still clinging hopelessly to the notion that somehow he would magically change back to the loving, caring man she once knew. She was convinced that this was just a phase their relationship was going through. I recognized that desperate look in her eyes. That was the same look I saw reflecting in the mirror so many times before. It was hard to try to convince someone of the truths it took you years to learn.

I often think about what would have happened if I had had someone to talk to, to guide me and help me break free. Would I have listened? Would I have believed what they were telling me? Sadly, I feel like the answer is no. These men are so charming and have a way of convincing you that their version of reality is the only truth. That they hurt you only because you made them. They cheated on you because you treated them badly. And you will start to believe it is all true.

You will start walking on eggshells, careful with your words, fearing anything you say or do will lead to a terrible consequence. I cut my own self off from a lot of family and friends under the guise of being very busy with work. It was easier than the hell I was sure to pay otherwise. From the outside, we looked like a picture-perfect couple. People were always commenting on how great we looked together or asking when the wedding would be. Little did they know what went on behind closed doors.

That's the thing about being in this type of abusive relationship. The marks left behind are not physical. Many people believe that it's not abuse if they do not hit you. There is no punishment for these types of abusers either. Even if there was, the narcissist would charm their way out of it. They would have the judge and jury convinced that the abused was to blame and that they were the victim. They're that good at what they do.

You can be well educated, smart, confident and so sure that you will never be "dumb enough" to fall for one of these types. I know I thought I was smarter than that. I didn't think I would fall for such a monster. The thing is, you don't fall for the monster of a man. You fall for the charming gentleman that wooed and courted you in the beginning. The one that fed you lies and everything that you wanted to hear in order to get closer to you. Every "I love you" and "we're meant for each other" was one step closer to getting you wrapped around their finger and twisted reality. So there you are, freshly in love and convinced you and this man are it—you found your forever man. You are so lucky to be with him—he's charming, handsome—just your perfect man. He makes you feel special. He says and does all the right things. You start imagining your whole lives together.

Then one day, out of the blue, he is upset about something you did. Maybe you don't even know what you said or did to upset them. You stand there, bewildered about what you possibly could have done to upset the love of your life. You didn't do anything wrong though. Please remember that. It was never your fault, no matter what they say. This is when they start their transformation into who they really are. This is when you may get your first real instinct that something is wrong, a major red flag.

You will defend yourself, knowing the truth and that you are not the liar or the cheater or whatever thing they are accusing you of.

This is the beginning of the vicious cycle. They will build you up with little bits of happiness only to tear you back down with their lies. It's disgusting how they will give you just enough hope to hold onto. Damage like that takes so much longer to heal than a bruise ever could.

One day, you will realize that the only way out is to get away. Find your freedom. It has been years since I have been in this type of relationship and I am still dealing with the aftermath. I know the emotional wounds will heal and the mental scars will fade someday.

Just learn from the past. Don't go for the same men. Break the cycle. Be free.

—*Lindsay J.*

LETTING GO

IN THE BEGINNING I WAS naïve. Naïve in the sense that I had never heard the term nor had the knowledge that there was a disorder called narcissism. Throughout my entire life I had been surrounded by good, caring, loving people. My parents provided an example of what true love, compassion, kindness and complete unselfishness was in a marriage and as parents of three children. The friends I associated with came from similar backgrounds.

As an adult, those relationships flourished. I went on to make new friends and eventually worked in an environment where I encountered a variety of people. I was married fourteen years to a good man who eventually lost himself to addiction. Not once in my thirty-two years had I encountered a truly evil person. That changed the day I said "I do" to my second husband, a narcissist. After five years of marriage, I learned how evil a person can be, but I also learned how strong I could be.

As with any narcissist, I encountered the love-bombing stage before we got married, and it continued throughout the first year of marriage. I was lavished with attention, time, compliments, gifts and love. When we were together he was extremely interested in me and how I felt about various things. Being naïve, I saw his actions as a genuine sign of his love without any indication I was actually being conned.

It was not until we divorced that I learned his "genuine interest" was a tool that he used to seek admiration from me, as well as a way to discover my weaknesses. Weaknesses he would later use to manipulate, control and ultimately hurt me.

This was my first "a-ha moment" as I looked back and recalled the types of things we talked about. I saw him for what he was: a con man. I was his prey, nothing more. He needed me to believe he was interested, that he cared about my feelings and loved me completely. He did this so I would give him the admiration he so deeply craved. I thought I found someone to be completely open and honest with, while he only looked to fulfill his own selfish need. I shared private things and feelings I had never shared with anyone else. Those expressions became his weapon once he lost the excitement from the newness of our relationship.

The second year of marriage I slowly began to see a different person emerge. He started to criticize me for the things he said he loved about me in the beginning. He criticized my weight, yet I was thin. At first he approached this topic in such a way it did not hurt. He would say things like, "Come work out with me so I can spend time with you." Over the next few years his comments became more personal, more hurtful. He criticized what I ate. He started purchasing all the food so he could control what my children and I consumed.

If I ate anything he considered inappropriate, I was criticized in private and eventually in front of others. I felt like I was going crazy! How did this person go from being so attracted to me to being so critical of me when my appearance had not changed from the first time we met?

The day after I gave birth to our daughter, I was asked, "Why are you still fat?" I cried. I was humiliated and what should have been a joyous occasion and a happy memory was tarnished. Eventually, I never felt comfortable in my own skin. I was self-conscious and confused. I did not understand how a person could tell me he loved me, show me that love physically, and sometimes emotionally, but on occasion be so cruel that it damaged anything I perceived as good in our relationship. I discovered that from his point of view, there really was no relationship, and the only thing that was good was what he took from me to make himself feel good.

Over the next few years, I began to see how things had to go his way all the time. He would lie about things we had agreed on and change them to fit his own intentions. Everything was always my fault. I was stupid, crazy, and immature. In the beginning I stood up for myself, but I would get punished with silent treatments for days or weeks at a time, no physical expressions of any kind or something would be taken from me.

I worked for his business and he controlled all the money. I was made to account for every penny I spent, but he did not have to answer to anyone. My position in his company was used as a way to further control me. Eventually, I gave up. I learned to pick and choose my battles because some things were not worth the retaliation. I became a person who walked on eggshells.

If I were to write down every bizarre, cruel thing my husband did to me over five years, I would have volumes of pages written of his horrific deeds— things no one should ever have to encounter from someone who says "I love you." To say it plainly, I lived in hell.

The biggest "a-ha moment" came when my sixteen-year-old daughter said, "Mom, I like it when he is gone because you are your old self." This was a huge eye-opener for me. I began to realize how much I enjoyed him being gone on business trips and that I did not look forward to his return. I had been lost. I was my former self when he was not around. I could relax without anyone criticizing me for the smallest things. I did not walk on eggshells when he was gone. I felt free. I knew it was time to leave because I wanted that feeling of freedom on a daily basis.

I ended up leaving the marriage in July of 2009 with no job, twenty dollars to my name, a limited amount of time to live in my home and three children to care for. Despite those obstacles, I was happier than I had been in a long time. I was free. Free to make my own choices, free from ridicule, free to enjoy life on a day-to-day basis.

I could return to me, the person I was before I met him, the fun-loving, positive girl. However, that feeling lasted for a fleeting moment before the sinking hit when I realized I would not have complete freedom because he used our daughter to continue his manipulation. She was his weapon of choice. The daughter he wanted to put up for adoption when I was seven months pregnant, and never showed any attention to while we were married unless other people were around that he wanted to impress.

Now that we were no longer married, he did not need anything from me to fix his need for admiration. He was as mean as ever, telling lies about me, saying I was the one who was abusive and that I stole his money. I was blessed to have the support of family and friends that knew the truth and never believed a word he said. Some victims are not so lucky. My biggest salvation came from a strange place: my decision to go to college.

Being forty and a single mother makes it hard enough for most people to go to school, but on top of all that, I was dealing with someone who was so evil that my life was worse than when I was married to him. I became overwhelmed and discouraged, wondering how I was going to cope with his treatment of my daughter and me until she was eighteen (she was only two when we divorced). My salvation came from the decision to go to a counselor at the university, where I learned that my ex was a narcissist, that term I had never heard of before.

I ended up writing a research paper on narcissism. Between the counselor and writing the paper, I learned so much about narcissism that it shed a whole new light on what I had lived through. In a sense, it gave me a feeling of freedom. I understood why I lived through hell with this person. I now had the knowledge that it had nothing to do with me and had everything to do with him and his sick way of feeding off of the goodness of others, the goodness of me.

The "goodness of me" became my motto.

I chose to no longer let him destroy the goodness in me. I continued therapy and learned how to set boundaries for myself, to keep a limited amount of contact, and only on issues concerning my daughter. However, trying to co-parent with a narcissist is difficult, so I pick and choose my battles. He still tries to control, but I use the law behind my divorce decree to protect me. I assert my rights to defeat his controlling games. I do not argue with him and I stick to the topic. It was a very hard thing to learn. I do not have to prove myself to him, I do not have to prove his lies are false, and arguing with him only feeds his manipulation. Once I learned this, I became free.

Six years later we are all doing well. My older kids are happy, healthy, functioning adults. My younger daughter is taught that her dad's behavior is not her fault, and she goes to therapy. She knows she is truly loved in my home and that she is always allowed to be herself and express her feelings, which she is not allowed to do at her dad's house.

I pray that my influence and her continued therapy will help her grow into a functioning, healthy, happy adult. I graduated from college with a 3.8 GPA and honors. I have a job at a university that I absolutely love.

We may not be completely free from the narcissist for a few more years, but I have learned to be free by not allowing him to affect me and by limiting my contact with him. By letting go, I am free!

I am a different person now. I am wiser and stronger for being married to a narcissist. I am a survivor, and that is amazing. I now have the ability to laugh at his behavior and the ability to recognize my own self-worth.

—Lynette Johnson

THE EMOTIONAL TERRORIST

FROM THE VERY BEGINNING OF my and Greg's relationship, it was a roller-coaster. It was passionate and exhilarating. He would constantly say how much he loved me, how thankful he was to have me, how wonderful I am and that he couldn't be without me. He thought the world of me. Being with him felt like a high; it felt so good, I craved it. As time went on, occasionally there would be instances where Greg would do something that made me feel uneasy... whether it was his too-close-for-comfort relationship with his female best friend, texting an ex, or disappearing a few days without contacting me; this would make me feel more anxious than I was used to feeling. If I'm so important to him, and he loves me so much, why can't I hold his attention? Why is he on Facebook right now commenting on other people's statuses, while I haven't heard from him in two days? After the fact, Greg would always reassure me of how much he loved me, have an excuse for his behavior and apologize to me, say that I shouldn't worry about him, and go on about how irreplaceable I was. He was so genuine and believable, I trusted him, and I forgave him.

Though I didn't see it at the time, I was slowly losing sight of myself, and I was also losing my confidence. I would anxiously await a text or phone call from Greg; I needed to hear from him. I tried harder and harder to be the best girlfriend I could be, thinking to myself, "If I was good enough, he would appreciate me. It's something I could be doing better." A year went by, and though our relationship was still passionate, it gave me a great deal of anxiety. It happened more often that he would do something to disrespect me and our relationship. Soon after, he would confess his love to me, reassuring me that it was an honest mistake.

A year into our relationship, on Monday, November 11, 2013, I found out that I was pregnant. Monday and Tuesday, he was extremely loving and reassuring. On Wednesday, he and I went to my first prenatal doctor's appointment. The doctor gave me two pregnancy tests; one test came up positive, one came up negative. He said to me that if I ended up not being pregnant, he would "run out the door and never look back."

I was shocked. How could Greg love me so much yesterday, and hate me today? What did I do wrong? I tried even harder to earn his approval and love. I felt blindsided. All of a sudden, from then on, he was an entirely different person to me. He sparingly showed me love and appreciation. He claimed that I was the reason for all of his anger, I made him miserable, and I made him so furious that he began calling me awful names that he never did before. He was telling my friends how controlling and uncompromising I was, that I needed to change, I treated him badly, and that he needed to get out. He was telling his own friends all about how awful I was, so they too were convincing him to leave me. The day before I found out I was having a baby girl, on Valentine's Day 2014, he changed his phone number because he wanted me out of his life.

After that, I was devastated. I was sick. I was emotionally and physically sick. All that I could think of was, "It's Valentine's Day, I'm halfway through my pregnancy, and the person I love wants nothing to do with me." I've never felt so low. I couldn't function without him. What was so wrong with me that the love of my life walked out on me when I needed him most? We're having a baby together, what did I do that made him so angry with me? I prayed, bargained, and wished for him to come back in to my life. I couldn't focus on anything. I ended up failing my college courses that semester, and I lost my job. I felt worthless. He didn't make me feel secure when he was in my life, but I felt insecure and like I had nothing without him. Talking to him and being with him was a high for me; it was everything I needed. Once we weren't together, I felt empty. I craved him, I needed him to function.

A couple of weeks later in March, he texted me from his new number saying that he missed me, loved me, and wanted to work things out. He invited me over to talk and spend time together that Saturday. It felt so good to talk to him, to be with him. It was wrong; I knew I shouldn't be treated that way by anyone. But I needed it. I was sick without him. It felt like I was in withdrawal. I went to spend time with him that Saturday, and it was exhilarating. He suggested I come back over Monday so we could talk about baby plans and the future. I sadly said goodbye and left to go home. Though everything was now good between us, I still felt a sense of emptiness. I felt euphoric when I was with him, but then felt empty and a deep sense of loneliness when I wasn't. I anxiously anticipated Monday.

Monday morning, I rushed to get ready and arrive at his house. I got there and the door was unlocked, so I let myself in. I called for him, but no answer. I went upstairs into his bedroom, and knocked on the door. It was locked. I asked why he locked me out of his bedroom, and he told me to go away. I started asking questions: "Why do you want me to leave? What's going on? Please just talk to me." He stormed out of the room, hurried me down the stairs and screamed in my face that he wanted nothing to do with me and to go home ... I noticed an unfamiliar purse and shoes in the corner of the living room. "Why do you want me to leave? Something's up, are you hiding something, or someone?" He said no, and said to check the house. I went back up into the bedroom, and noticed that a "blanket" was breathing in the closet. My heart was pounding out of my chest, there's no way he's hiding a girl in his closet ... I yanked the blanket, and there lay a half-naked girl. I wanted to die. How could he do this to me?! I ran out of the house as fast as I could, and drove away. How could he ask me to come over on Monday at this time, and have me walk in on that? He set me up. He was an emotional terrorist.

Words aren't powerful enough to explain the despair I felt. He had a hold over me. I blocked his number, and did my best to cut off all contact with him. I vowed to myself that I needed to remove this toxic relationship from my life, regardless of the cost. It was killing me. I felt like I was an addict going through withdrawal without him, but somehow I persevered one agonizing day at a time. I had to break my addiction to him. Our daughter Leanna was born on July 8, 2014. I negotiated with his parents to coparent through them, rather than him. Cutting him out entirely was the only way to suck the poison out of my life.

Fast forward to today: It is October 2015. After a violent outburst involving our daughter, I was able to file a Protection from Abuse case against him, and I haven't had contact with him in months. Since I cut him out of my life, his life has spiraled out of control. My life has been exponentially getting better, and nothing gives me more satisfaction than knowing that he's watching it all from the outside. His car got repossessed the same day our daughter was born. Not too long after that, he was charged with corrupting minors and drug paraphernalia. The girl I found in his closet gave him chlamydia, and ended up terrorizing his life. I met an incredible man 9 months ago named James, who I have been in a healthy, nurturing relationship with ever since. Coincidentally, James lives on the same street as Greg's workplace. Every day on Greg's way to and from work, he gets to see my car parked at another man's house. He no longer has a hold on me. He no longer controls me. I am free.

Since my experience, I have felt compelled to help other people gain insight and control of their lives. Doing so, I have been pursuing my dreams as a psychologist, and I will be finished with college within the next year. My confidence is gradually coming back, and I am finally my happy, high-achieving self again. I didn't think there was a life beyond Greg and the agony I felt with him in my life. To anyone suffering through a situation like this: do not give up hope. Keep pushing through. You are strong; you are an incredible person despite what the narcissist had you believing. I couldn't have imagined how perfect my life could be within just two years of how awful things were before. I got my life back. I am free.

—*Kelsey Chizmar*

FINDING CLOSURE

I HAD NO IDEA THAT as my long hair swished to the sound of his dreamy, laid-back guitar strums, I was beginning a dark and stormy chapter of my life at the age of eighteen.

College had just begun and I was eager to see what it had in store for me. I had completed a sobering, yet completely foreign experience of new student orientation, where domestic violence was discussed as one of the topics. During the presentation we were asked to raise our hands if we thought we would be able to leave a relationship after the first sign of abuse and also be able to speak clearly about it. Among the 98 students present, 85 raised their hands, myself included. Little did I know how difficult it actually was to leave an abusive situation and to express what had happened to the proper authorities.

Leaning back in his chair in his untidy room that was scattered with stacks of engineering paperwork in his fraternity house, he seemed carefree, intelligent, and spirited. I was immediately drawn to all that he appeared to embody. I'd never had a boyfriend for more than a week, so I was naïve about how adult relationships were supposed to progress.

I did not have the ideal family background, as I come from a line of sociopaths and narcissists. The "normal people" in my family had to scrounge for salvation in one form or another. I thought going away to college would be my salvation. Little did I know I would find the same miserable type of people just waiting for their next victims to surface.

A few months passed as I hoped that I could be his girlfriend. He was kind and thoughtful, surprising me with flowers, my favorite snacks, and a song that expressed his adoration of me. I was smitten. The night he asked me to be his girlfriend was anything but romantic. He had me over to his fraternity and forced me to have sex with him. He said it was the only way to make sure this was going to work. I undressed and lost my virginity because I did not know that was not how it was supposed to be. In the heat of the moment, he asked me to be his girlfriend. At the time I could not identify his actions as sexual aggression and mistook it for passion.

I should have recalled the domestic violence presentation and my belief that I would leave a relationship should I encounter abuse, but I did not know that this was abuse. When issues would crop up, whether they were a disagreement mentally, emotionally, or sexually, I always expected myself to fix it, as I had done with my family members.

When he did not get his way he would throw himself on the ground and cry until he fell asleep. He would blame me for things I could not control. He would do the opposite of what I asked of him. He used sleep as a form of dismissing me, ignored my cries for help, and convinced me to hate my friends and family, while letting his friends and family abuse me further. He lied to those close to him about me often and painted me to be a villain. His mom would frequently send me derogatory messages and try to force me into marrying her son, as that was the only way she would recognize our relationship in her conservative mind. After a year and a half of blaming myself, I finally sought external support.

I went to see a therapist to discuss my relationship and to see if it was salvageable. He confirmed my worst fear: I was dating a narcissist and a sociopath. We discussed the details of the relationship and at the conclusion, my therapist bluntly stated, "You need to leave him immediately before it gets worse. This is abuse and you will not live the life you want."

It was hard for me to realize that our relationship was false and driven by his need to be elusive and selfish. He hid behind his family and his fraternity, with consistently changing stories. He convinced me that I was the problem, that I was worthless, that I would be nothing. He didn't understand why I was working so hard to succeed in school since I was going to be a trophy wife anyway. I still did not identify and accept the signs of abuse until my therapist said, "Leave him."

Later that day I told him what the therapist said. He immediately lashed out in anguish and blamed me for being insecure. I asked him to fix five fundamental issues in our relationship: compassion, communication, respect for each other and our home, respect for my requests, and to live with honest conviction. Instead of agreeing and doing whatever it took to keep our relationship afloat, he threw a fit, cried, and ignored me for six days.

The abuse did not end there. He changed the truth of what happened, framing me as the abuser and painting me in a derogatory light to his family and to his fraternity. His fraternity brothers adopted his narcissistic and sociopathic behaviors and directed them toward me. They objectified me and treated me with utter disrespect that ended in sexual, emotional, and physical violence. Their narcissism led them to believe that they were protected by their fraternity, their youth, and their college. They lied to protect themselves and created a hostile and unsafe environment for me to be in. His family knew to leave me alone.

For the most part, this chapter in my life is over. The college will soon make a decision regarding disciplinary actions on the fraternity as a whole. I can finally rest. If I could do everything again, I would not be afraid to report the abuse to the proper people. While we cannot completely end situations like this, awareness can help others recognize and prevent that kind of behavior in ourselves and in our relationships.

The hardest part of this journey was finding the words to express what happened and the emotions that I felt. Since abusers typically tell their victims that the abuse is their fault, it is difficult not to blame yourself. More often than not, these types of aggressors will target good-hearted and trusting people who will believe them.

Finding closure was also challenging. Initially, I felt like I betrayed myself and the promises I made to keep my body, heart, and mind safe. I was filled with regret and blame, but came to realize that those were residual feelings left from individuals that abused me.

When I finally understood that I could not have possibly controlled what happened to me, I was proud to say that I did the right thing.

The words and relief came to me when I realized that I was free.

—*Alexandra Sarell*

SCORCHED EARTH

I NEVER KNEW THAT THE problems in my relationship with my now ex-husband were caused by / classified as narcissism or abuse. Even after I started reading about this I didn't believe that I was actually abused because he never physically hurt me. As recently as eight months ago I was asked by an attorney appointed to my children as a guardian ad litem if I was ever abused and I mistakenly answered "no." Since I have started to educate myself though it has made a WORLD of difference in how I look at the past 15 years and how it has changed me.

The first times that any of this ever came up it was subtle and he laughed it off. He loved to cut me down in front of friends and then pretend that it was all just a joke. One time I had a different opinion than his on the reliability of a type of car and he snapped, "What the f*** do you know about cars anyway?" Only when the room was silent did he realize he had overstepped and pretended he was joking. This never stopped although he did adjust his behavior to only belittle me in front of his family and friends and not before mine as much. Of course it helped that after a while I no longer had many friends around.

I was never able to do anything right. He believed that he had to teach me everything. According to him, I didn't even know how to boil water properly. Seriously. He felt he had to teach me how to boil water! At the time, I chalked this up to our age difference. He was thirteen years my senior and graciously explained to me that through his experience, I could learn a thing or two. Apparently that even included rudimentary cooking skills.

Any time we had an argument or I tried to bring up something about the relationship that I was unhappy with he would immediately bring up a short-coming of mine (that usually had nothing to do with what we were talking about). I called this his "I know you are but what am I?" argument. To say he acted like a spoiled five-year-old is an insult to five-year-olds because his behavior was so much worse. If I was ever to get anything in the relationship without a fight I had to flip things around to make him believe it was his idea and then praise him for being so ingenious. It made me sick.

One of his favorite things to do in an argument would be to tell me how incapable I was of admitting when I was wrong, and then he would sarcastically apologize. Later he would tell me he was never sorry; he would only say it because he would "rather be happy than right." It was just one more way he had of making himself the bigger person than me because I was so incapable of humbling myself before him.

He always considered himself smarter than everyone else and was frequently unemployed because no one could stand having him around for long. I supported us for the vast majority of our relationship. No matter how often he was fired, there was never any disappointment or a single moment of self-blame. It was always someone else's fault. Someone always had it out for him. His boss just couldn't handle working with him anymore because the boss just felt too inferior to him. He was so awful at one state job that he was placed on a permanent no-hire list for the entire state where we lived. All of this happened when he started abusing prescription pills again and preceded what was to be a colossal relapse into drug and alcohol abuse.

When we met, my ex was a recovering alcoholic and had one year clean. He often wanted me to accompany him to AA meetings with him or go to Al-Anon meetings on my own. I am not saying that these programs are not extremely beneficial but all they served to do for me was to shine an even bigger light on the problems in our relationship and the fact that even though he was not drinking, going to these meetings wasn't helping any of his underlying character flaws. He was unwilling to ever honestly admit that he had personal issues with control and feelings of superiority. He was extremely good at saying all the right things and putting on the costume of a humble, honest, caring individual but behind closed doors there was no one he needed to perform for. For him, going to those meetings was a waste of time. He thoroughly believed that I needed Al-Anon though so that I could make myself better for him.

Despite all of this craziness, after dating for four years, we decided to get married. We were both just beginning our graduate degrees and going to school in separate states with a six-hour drive between us but for some reason marriage seemed like a great idea at the time. Ridiculous. I arranged my classes so that I could travel to see him practically every weekend. He only came to see me three times in three years. One time was a middle-of-the-night surprise visit because he was convinced I was cheating on him. Of course I wasn't.

While in school, he was supposed to live and care for my parents' home—rent free—after they retired and moved away. This would enable them to keep the house instead of selling it (they didn't want to rent it out and the house couldn't just stand empty), something he knew that I desperately wanted because I loved my childhood home. Without telling me, he rented a trailer 20 minutes closer to school because he just "wouldn't have been able to handle the drive to school every day." And for the sake of 40 minutes per day, my parents sold their home. He thought that I was histrionic and irrational when I came unglued over that one. He knew exactly what he was doing, which was why he rented the new place in secret and he never even apologized for it.

Fast-forward several years to 2009. We had both graduated. I found a great job and he was still constantly searching for work.

In March I gave birth to our first child, a boy. I used to tell my ex that someday he would be sorry when I no longer tried to hold his hand or give him hugs and beg for affection. When my son came into my life, that day finally came for him. From the minute I held my son, he was my everything. He was the most perfect being I had ever seen and I would never be the same. Suddenly nothing my ex did or didn't do mattered. I no longer cared if he loved me or respected me or thought I was smart or pretty. I had someone in my life that I would give my last breath to protect and love. It was the most overwhelmingly strong feeling I have ever felt.

Unfortunately, the time came when I had to head back to work. Since he was unemployed and we were terribly broke, my ex stayed home with our son. On July 13, 2009, when my son was just shy of four months old, I called home and heard my son screaming in the background. When I asked what was wrong with the baby he nonchalantly answered that he fell off of the kitchen table but he was fine. I later learned that my ex had put him in his bouncy chair on the kitchen table and then left the room to do something in another part of the house. Through his movements, my son then gradually bounced the chair right off of the table. My ex was not at all concerned with this and said "the kid is fine." I told him to meet me at the hospital immediately. I arrived at the emergency room first and was standing outside on the sidewalk when he pulled up. He had not even bothered to secure the infant carrier into the base in the back of his car. As he pulled around in front I saw the baby and the carrier roll completely over in the backseat and the baby was screaming louder than I had ever heard him scream in his short life.

After X-rays, CT scans, and a life-flight helicopter ride to a nearby children's hospital, I learned that my son had a skull fracture. To say I was furious is such an understatement. Through all of this, my ex never expressed remorse, guilt, sadness or any of the feelings that any normal parent would express knowing that something they did caused a serious injury to their child. The only thing he ever said to me was, "If the shoe had been on the other foot and this happened when you were watching him, I would never go out of my way to try to make you feel bad about it."

After this "accident," I considered divorce for the first time but I was terrified. I knew that at best I could expect the ex to get every other weekend with my defenseless child with no one to look out for him. Because I knew that I could never leave him alone with the ex again, I stayed. And even though it was a financial struggle, I found a full-time babysitter for my son where I knew he would be well cared for. There is no way of proving that the accident that happened to my son wasn't just an accident but I have always suspected that wasn't the case. My ex was extremely jealous of our son and that has not changed all through the years. My son is almost 7 now and is unfortunately having his own struggles and issues with his father as a result of his dad's narcissism.

In December 2009, I began to have symptoms of arthritis but they went undiagnosed for years. I went to various doctors and had surgeries on my hand but got no help at home. After my first surgery, we had a massive snowstorm that dumped several feet of snow. My ex refused to shovel the sidewalks or the driveway. I went out with my hand bandaged a day after surgery and shoveled the sidewalk. When I could do no more, my 64-year-old mother, who had come to stay to help with the baby, shoveled the driveway. My ex did nothing. This is a man who would not even help me bathe when I couldn't wash my hair by myself after surgery and I expected him to valiantly take up a snow shovel and dig us out? Please.

Our marriage continued this way and I got quite accustomed to doing everything on my own. I didn't even bother asking him for anything anymore. He finally found a job working with at-risk youth but trouble started with that position almost immediately. Everyone was out to get him again and caused him so much stress that he had to take family medical leave for three months, unpaid. In the middle of this, I had our second child—this time a gorgeous little girl.

When I was six months pregnant, my ex reported to me that he had been abusing over-the-counter cold medicine. Can you believe that is even a thing? Supposedly he had been taking drug tips from the youth he was supposed to be supervising because getting high on massive doses of cough medicine was the hot thing to do for teenagers. He checked himself in to the VA Medical Center and got himself dried out for a couple of days, refused to stay for long-term in-patient treatment even though I wanted him to, and came home like nothing had ever happened. There was never an apology or a promise that he would be better. Nothing.

While I was in the hospital after having my daughter, my ex showed up so high that I couldn't believe that he had the nerve to walk in the hospital like that. His eyes were bloodshot and glassy; he was sweating and barely able to walk. I no longer cared how embarrassed he made me. I told him how much I appreciated him coming to the hospital high and giving me that wonderful memory of my daughter's birth to look back on. I learned later that he had gone to a local urgent care known for passing out pain killers like tic tacs and gave them a sob story about how awful his back pain was. When we came home with my daughter, who I delivered via C-section, I discovered my prescription painkillers were all gone. I had just had a human being removed from my body and he took my painkillers! I told him that I would not have my children living with an addict; I didn't care what he was on. If it happened again, I was done. Apparently, he thought I was kidding.

When my daughter was eight months old, I found more empty cold medicine boxes with a receipt dated the same day. That. Was. It. When he came back to the house I told him what I had found; of course he tried denying it, saying they were old, telling me I was crazy, blah, blah, blah. This time nothing he said worked. I was done. I told him either he was leaving or I was. When I started packing our things it dawned on him I was serious and he left. Now comes the colossal bender. I didn't hear from him for days. He abandoned his teenage daughter from his first marriage at our home for me to care for, which I did because it wasn't her fault her father was a nightmare. Unfortunately, she had her own troubles and eventually went to stay with friends (at her father's insistence) because his family would not take her in until he came out of rehab.

The weekend my ex left I cleaned out the house of every belonging he had. I rented a storage building in his name and put every box, bag and book he had in it. There was nothing left of his when I was done. It was called Operation Scorched Earth. I left no trace of him. I had never been so upset or so exhilarated. I had my life back. I had my house back. I no longer had someone telling me I was wrong or crazy, or stupid. No one to tell me that I made him walk on eggshells because of how much stress I put on him. For the first time in ten years I was alone again and I was THRILLED. I could finally do anything I wanted in my own home without begging and explaining and justifying and I was never going back.

Eventually he ended up in the hospital (he has a heart condition that he takes blood thinners for and was drinking massive amounts of alcohol, not a good combo.) He was stabilized and released. I would not allow him back to my home and I told him I had filed for divorce. He went on another bender. This time he rented a hotel room and holed himself in there drinking gallons, yes gallons, of vodka. When I located him at the hotel all he would say to me is that he "never would have done this" to me, meaning divorce. He still saw nothing wrong with tearing our family apart, abandoning all three of his children or hurting me without a second thought. It was all still only about him and his feelings.

I then did the only thing in my life that I can look back at with real regret. If I could change any action in my life it would be this: I poured out his liquor bottles, I took all of his credit cards and ID and I drove him to the VA hospital. His family refused to help me. No one cared what happened to him anymore. When we got there, his blood alcohol was .362. I had a moment standing in that filthy hotel room where I could have just turned and walked out the door. He was hours away from killing himself with alcohol and all of my future problems would be totally avoidable. I knew that someday I would regret helping him. Someday I would wish with almost everything I had to go back in time and make myself walk out the door and do nothing to help him. I knew standing there though that I had to do something so that I could one day tell my children that I did everything I could to help their father even when I knew, deep down, that he wasn't worth helping.

As a result of the divorce, I got full custody and he had visits at my discretion. A better outcome than I could've hoped for. I allowed him to come to my home to visit with the kids to keep things as normal for them as possible. Always, my only thoughts are what is best for them. It made my skin crawl to have him in my home again but I am an adult in control of my feelings and my feelings come second to that of my children. He eventually screwed up being permitted at my home by showing up intoxicated. He refused to help my son when his fingers were slammed in his car door, another "accident." Then he passed out on my living room floor and I could barely get him out of the house. He didn't see the kids for months after that because he was whacked out on who knows what substance at that point.

When he finally did see them again he let my two-year-old daughter run out in front of a car and then yelled at her for not being careful. During one visit, they were at a mall where my daughter wandered off and he never even noticed. All of this happened when he was sober. He is dangerously inattentive to our children and got angry when I wouldn't let him see them without me there. The visits grew shorter and shorter with more and more time between them. He expected me to drop everything and meet him with a moment's notice rather than set up visits ahead of time, as I asked him to do repeatedly. At one visit, he allowed my son to run across a busy, ice-covered parking lot where my son fell and slid partway under my vehicle. When I told him to be more careful he came unglued and screamed at me in front of the children. Both kids were upset and no longer wanted to see him. It took me months to get my son comfortable with seeing his dad again and even then I had to force him to a visit at the park. Twenty minutes into the visit, my son begged to go home because of a stomachache and he promptly threw up in the car on the way home. He can't stand seeing his dad and begs me all the time not to make him go. The ex claims that I am making my kids crazy and stressing them out and that is why they get sick and don't want to be with him. It is totally beyond his comprehension that is simply him they don't want to be around and that I have nothing to do with it.

After the last visit at the park, I refused to put my son through any more visits until he was ready. I have been told that I should have made my kids go whether they wanted to or not because they don't have a choice about seeing their dad. I have never been able to understand how forcing a child to spend time with a person that they are frightened of is going to build a relationship.

So after months of threats, my ex sent me papers last Christmas that he was suing me for custody modification. That was a planned jab right at the holidays. He didn't even file the papers with the court until the middle of January but he had to send me those right at Christmas so that he could attempt to ruin yet another holiday. We have had a bitter custody battle all year. My son, who is now six, had to see a counselor and both children were appointed a guardian ad litem (a lawyer to represent their interests) by the court. I have had to watch my children be forced to see this man week after week. The visits started out as supervised, two hours a week—of which he only took one hour each week (even though he complained incessantly of never getting to see his kids).

The guardian ad litem, who was supposed to be on my kids' side, never even interviewed my kids a single time. When it came time to give a report to the court, she did so before even visiting my ex's house to see if it was suitable. My children didn't even have beds to sleep in but she thought that was A-OK! She determined that my ex should start getting unsupervised visitation on weekend days to work up to overnights over a period of weeks. My ex was supposed to pick up my son from school one day to take him to a counseling appointment and he forgot him. My son was the only one left at school when I was notified that my ex never showed up. My son told me, "I thought I was going to have to sleep there." When I spoke to the guardian about this she said, "You know, I was really upset when he did that. Here he has two people working so hard to give him everything he wants and he goes and does something stupid like that." So instead of the counselor and the guardian looking out for my children, now I knew that all they were doing was trying to put a rubber stamp on my ex as a perfect father. To make matters worse, when I would try to explain to everyone how dangerous he was to my kids, my own attorney and the guardian ad litem both told me that I was the one who decided to have kids with him.

My son's counselor said that he had been playing with a mommy and daddy doll during a session and she thought it was very telling that he started hitting the daddy doll with the mommy doll and decided that I was saying inappropriate things to my child about his father. It never occurred to anyone that my son was angry about his father mistreating me, mistreating him, telling my children that they were only allowed to love him, forgetting him at school or any number of other things. None of that fit the way they wanted things to work out in all of our lives. But guess what did? Parental alienation! Now after years of mistreatment, but yet still allowing this man to come to my home to see our children and bending over backwards to do the right thing at every turn, I was being accused of turning my children against him. He had no culpability whatsoever in the way our children feel about him. He was nothing but an innocent victim of my war on fatherhood. All of the times that my son screamed and begged not to go with his dad, all of the times he ran into his closet and hid so he wouldn't have to go, all of the times that he asked me if he could just pretend he was asleep so he wouldn't have to go didn't matter. No one listened to him but me, and I was powerless to do anything.

As if all of this wasn't enough, my son came home from his last visit with his father and reported that he had been grabbed and held up by one arm so that his feet barely touched the floor and spanked. My ex left a bruise on his wrist and he complained of pain there for two days. I thought and I thought about what to do and after a very sleepless night and praying until I couldn't pray anymore I decided to take my son to see the police. He told them exactly what happened and the officer took pictures of his bruise and then filed domestic battery charges against my ex. They advised me to get a protective order, which I did. The judge that heard the case for the protective order was the same judge hearing our custody case. I had heard a lot of horror stories about this woman but you never truly believe things are that bad until you are forced to witness them yourself.

My protective order was denied and I was accused of manipulating the criminal justice system all because I checked the wrong box on one form. I was told by my son's counselor that she wished I had talked to her before the police because she would have told me not to report the incident because she knew that the judge would hold it against me. The following week we had our final custody hearing and the judge accused me of alienating the kids from their father and that all the criminal charges were just a part of my plot. She told me if she could she would take more time with my children away from me. She sarcastically asked the guardian ad litem if I was even capable of learning how to be a good mother. She gave my ex legal advice from the bench on how to beat his criminal charges. She gave him all the visitation that he wanted.

I walked out of that courtroom completely shell shocked. I could not believe what had happened over the past nine months. I could not believe that none of these "learned professionals" were intelligent enough to see through this act that he is the victim. Every time he would do something, like leaving my son at school, I would think, "Finally! They will all see what I've been talking about!" But all they would do is make excuses for him and pretend it never happened.

I saw the absolute worst of the family court system during my case. I started to lose my faith because it didn't seem to matter how hard I prayed for God to help my children, things just got worse. I now believe that my prayers were answered, just not the way I had hoped. I had to see how bad things were and the misery that I had heard about from other families was not only true but worse than I could've ever imagined. I decided that I couldn't just sit back and let this happen to anyone else. I decided to run for family court judge and do my very best to take the job away from the woman who puts her personal agenda and feelings above the best interests of children. Most other people that have the misfortune of appearing before this judge are left only with the options to appeal—which often goes nowhere—or to report her for judicial ethics violations, which are so hard to prove that they also often go nowhere. I am in the best position to take action because I am an attorney and am more than qualified to take on the huge responsibility that comes with making decisions involving children.

As of this writing, my ex's criminal case is still pending. I got word yesterday that he has hired a local attorney, a colleague of mine, who is trying to get his no-contact bond condition lifted so that he may see the kids again. I continue to pray, and ask for prayers, for a light to be shown on this man and for all involved to see him without his mask. It took me years to see it but I am hoping, for my son's sake, a criminal judge and jury will see it much more quickly than

I did. I pray that someone will finally listen to my children without the callous assumption that they are simply parroting my feelings and thoughts.

For all of those going through their own difficult times with a narcissist, you are stronger than you know. You can handle this and get through it. You do not need to settle for this treatment. You are worth more than the narcissist is willing to give. Do not give him or her more power in your life—they feed off of it. If you have children, leave so they will not learn this behavior or become victims themselves. Be alone and find out how happy you will be for the first time in forever. Get away. Break ties. Scorch the Earth.

—Sabine McCloud

DESTINY

I REMEMBERED HOW I FELT, as if I was just holding my breath underwater and kept saying to myself, "Very soon I will break the surface and it will all be okay." But then ultimately it was not; it took too long before I could take my next breath of fresh air and I slowly started to drown. Drown in suppressed emotions.

It was not my destiny to be a victim of abuse. It was not what God had planned for my life. Even if it had been so for many years, it was not how I was going to end my life.

Nothing in my life ever seemed deliberately planned or structured, except how to stay safe and how to keep my children safe. I made a mistake as a child and was lured into a relationship with a predatory adult man and then it seemed like my inner and outer world conspired against me. When I wanted to get out I was trapped by guilt, circumstances and shame. I no longer had a mother or home to run back to for safety. I ended up married to what everyone believed was an honest and dignified young man.

There were not many choices left to me. I had only just turned eighteen. I bore him three children and constantly pushed down my feelings of shame, fear for my children, and fear for myself. The constant anxiety was taxing and yet it is not always easy just to "get out." There is the dynamic of an abuser systematically destroying your self-worth until you believe yourself to be incapable of doing anything and then when you do try to do something, you find you are not believed and the law of the country runs counter to the victim. When you want to get out, there is no one who can accommodate you and you lack the educational and financial means to support yourself and children. When I was still young and strong, I still had hope. Then I slowly started drifting in and out of psychiatric wards and I knew I was trapped forever. Who would grant me custody of my children when I could no longer take care of them? Where could I go but to the marital home to recover, only to be bullied and put back in a psychiatric ward?

I could no longer outrun my emotions. I had to stop. I knew it had to stop. I started watching the sunrise in the morning while everyone was still asleep. I would sit on the step outside and look out over the valley and listen to the birds slowly start to wake. The sunlight would slowly creep towards me across the valley until I felt the warmth of it on my face. The morning star would then be directly above my head and the sun would slowly nudge it out of the way until it disappeared over the horizon. It was the one time I was at peace and I could reflect.

With this peace eventually came the silence in my mind. I heard nothing but nature around me and the voices who whispered constantly of my distress became quiet as if they too were listening. Slowly my self-worth gained the strength I needed. Then with gentleness and unobtrusively, a new voice whispered in a new language of hope. It slowly silenced the anxious voice of worry. It was reminding me of how I was many years ago. When I was still a child. It reminded me of what I was capable of and how my life used to be. It placed before me the images of my life that I had forgotten and it made me smile in delight. I knew whose voice this was. It was mine. I was not lost. I was just hidden under all that burden of shame.

I knew what I needed to do: I had to strategize. No one was coming to rescue me—I had to rescue myself. I had to find a way in which I could leave this place. It might take time, but at least I would have tried.

I remembered my strengths and looked past those words that echoed like a sick refrain in my head: "You cannot organize a piss-up in a brewery." Who would want to do that anyway? Surely there were more important things I could do with my life.

Every morning I would sit and watch the sun come up and indulge myself in the new voice of reason that had started to speak a new truth. The voice had become stronger and it gave me encouragement after another bout of verbal abuse. It told me there is a door which is not locked and if I planned carefully I could slip out of it even if only in my mind and escape the terror of it all and remember who I was and what I can do. It would remind me of the dreams I used to have and that I could make them come true.

Fate opened a crack in the door: a better job with more financial rewards. No more salary being paid into the communal account, at least not all of it. I have learned to become sly. I will just keep most of it for myself and pay for my education without anyone even knowing.

I remember the day my first books arrived. I was beside myself with excitement and wanted to share this joy, yet I knew that it would only stoke the fire of his insecurity that I would one day leave. He did not love me, yet he did not want me to go. He had always had a brooding kind of mind, drawn within himself, never sharing anything of consequence. I had truly come to think there was nothing inside to share.

I watched him every morning getting ready for work. He would stand in front of the mirror and he would take his time. He was like an artist—never quite satisfied. He would step back and look at himself speculatively and I would watch. Only the best for him. The most expensive shoes. Only custom-made suits made from the most expensive fabric. Only the most expensive shirts. Getting dressed was a complete ritual, the constant turning after putting on each item to make sure it fits just right. I would puzzle about this and wonder why he was so extremely fussy. I never dressed in front of the mirror. I never had time for all this fussing.

It was not easy. I was constantly harassed to "come to bed" when I tried to study at night. I had three children who were amazingly talented in spite of our dysfunctional home. It did require hours of fetching and carrying and waiting in front of the schools. I learned to do my assignments balanced on my lap while waiting in front of schools.

The pressure bore down on me like a ton of bricks. I struggled and failed sometimes and had to redo a subject; then my studying went underground. I had to reassure him that I had abandoned the idea—his insecurity created too many problems and it became harder to stay out of harm's way.

A wider crack opened in spite of not having completed my first degree. I managed to fudge my way with smooth talking into teaching word processing at a university. The salary was such a leap. I saw the end of the road. I had stopped counting the years it was taking to try and study, maybe ten I was speculating.

I did not have the foggiest idea how the word processor worked or how to teach a subject I had not been fully trained for, but a force greater than myself just started placing opportunities in my path. There was a strike at the university. I did not hesitate. I borrowed the machine (that was long before computers) and set about learning at home. The strike lasted long enough to work it all out. By the time I went back, I knew how it worked.

The workload was extremely heavy and I had to learn along the way. My home situation had also changed. We had counseling to sort out the abuse. He turned it into having given me no more than a slap on the wrist, but he stopped and replaced it with just another form of abuse. Icy coldness. I decided to make it work for me. I now had a roof over my head and food on my table and essentially no husband. Suddenly I realized that it was an opportunity to continue my studies and complete them within two years. My children no longer needed my protection. Those two years flew by. I could not stop. I was hooked. It was not enough; I needed even more for my life. I moved departments to one more suited to my line of study.

The university would sponsor another degree. It was part of their employment policy. At times I sat and pondered how all of this was happening so fast and so smoothly. The first year into my master's and my first exam loomed. He knew where the venue was and to my surprise he suddenly turned up before the exam. He made sure to tell my colleague standing with me just how proud he was of me. I went into the exam and got 49%. I cried and cried and knew this was his next strategy. I had to move out. I had to divorce him. I had hoped to avoid this stress until my studies were done.

He insisted that I had to be declared "sane" before he would agree. The trauma of that experience and financial outcome in the end was so typical of him. He never played fair. Did I really expect anything less?

I completed my master's in record time. My supervisor could not believe it when he marked it. Fair enough not top marks for me. But it was done.

In the following eighteen years my destiny was solidified. I had discovered talents and gifts more than I could ever have dreamt of. By the time I retired I was financially secure. I had somehow through it all kept a positive spirit and developed a sense of humor.

I look back today and I know—destiny is like a spider's web. It is not a straight line from birth to your end. It is in and out of places and events and is part of the greater scheme of things. Just so, my life traveled into discovering my destiny. I experienced joy, happiness, challenges, and discovered something new every day and I know that it is by God's grace that it is so.

—*Felicity Botha*

WINDS OF FREEDOM

THE NIGHT BEFORE, I'D BEEN on the phone sobbing to a psychiatric social worker because I just couldn't take the verbal abuse from my boss anymore.

I'd done exactly as instructed and checked with one of the daycare teachers to see whether a handyman had finished putting up shelving in her classroom. I'd reported back to Paula that the teacher had said the job was complete. Paula asked me to go to the classroom and double-check, and, if the job was not done, she wanted me to stop the handyman from leaving and make sure he finished the task.

The shelving been put up, and the handyman had left.

When I reported this to Paula over the phone, she was furious. She insisted the job had not been completed: "Those shelves need to be bolted to the wall. I don't think they're bolted to the wall! You should have stopped him before he left."

Though I didn't say anything to Paula, I wondered two things: (1) Why couldn't she have been there to supervise the handyman if it was so important to her he complete the job to her specifications? and (2) Why was I was taking the brunt of her anger, when I'd never been told what those specifications were?

Paula demanded I call the handyman up and tell him to come back first thing the next day: the Veteran's Day holiday. She also demanded that I give up my holiday to supervise his work. I agreed to the first portion of her request, but not the second.

It was not my fault he hadn't finished the job, and I felt that Paula was singling me out for punishment and that it was not fair.

Paula sighed loudly and said fine, she'd come in the next morning to supervise the handyman, but her parting shot to me before she ended the phone call was, "Just so you know, I usually spend Veteran's Day in silent reflection because it is my dead mother's birthday."

I spent Veteran's Day not in silent reflection, but in a phone appointment and in emails back and forth with my psychiatrist. I'd been documenting everything to my doctor for months: work hours, crying spells, panic attacks, and yes, incidents of verbal abuse. He'd told me just a few weeks before that my current situation was unsustainable and bad for my health.

Around noon on Veteran's Day, after my email documenting the handyman incident, my doctor responded to say that this latest incident of verbal abuse should be my last. He advised me to quit immediately, and agreed he would write me a letter for the state unemployment office stating that the work environment at the daycare was contributing to an exacerbation of symptoms and was detrimental to my health.

That night was different from the night before, and from every night for the past 16 months since. No more crying because, yet again, I'd had to give up an evening, weekend, time with friends or family, interests outside of work to meet the demands of a narcissistic boss.

No more uncompensated overtime. No more unclear expectations and no more being berated when I hadn't met them. No more empty promises about a more reasonable work schedule, writing projects she was going to have me work on, or anything else she'd lied to me about to keep me from leaving. No more phone calls or emails from Paula either; I'd blocked her phone numbers and email addresses.

When I returned to the daycare for the last time on Veteran's Day night, it was dark and quiet. Paula's car was not in the parking lot. I unlocked the back door and turned on the light. There was a stack of green folders on my desk from the in-service training that weekend, with a note: "Marisa, before you get started on this project, let's talk."

I ignored the project and the note. They hadn't been on my desk the night before, and I had something more pressing to do. I filed away some paperwork I'd brought home with me to ensure it got done in time to meet Paula's unrealistic deadlines. Then I turned on my computer and pulled up in my work email my one-way ticket to freedom: the resignation letter I'd written earlier in the day and emailed to myself from home. All I had to do now was print out the letter and leave it with my keys on my desk. I could do this.

But panic gripped me like a vise. What if it was all just a misunderstanding and everything would be better tomorrow? What if Paula finally did follow through on some of those promises she made?

I couldn't let myself go down that road again. It had led me to the point, less than twenty-four hours ago, where I was thinking of committing suicide if I had to spend one more day working in that place.

In an attempt to calm myself, I logged on to Pandora—an act of rebellion in itself, since normally I wasn't allowed to play music in the office where I worked. What happened next, I can only say was a sign: The very first song that came on was "Ventura Highway" by America.

With a smile on my face, I printed out my resignation letter and put it, along with my keys, in an envelope addressed to Paula. I was strong in my belief that whatever awaited me outside those office walls, it had to be better than what I'd found inside them.

As I left that miserable place for the last time, hearing the click of the automatic lock on the door behind me, I was drunk on the power I'd just taken back for myself. And standing outside in the damp November chill, waiting for the bus, I could almost feel the winds of freedom blowing through my hair.

—*Marisa Wood*

THIRTY-YEAR CAPTIVITY

I MET AND MARRIED MY husband at the age of twenty-five, after only dating for a month. It seemed to be a match made in heaven. I was living at home at the time, had a horrible eating disorder, and was terribly lonely and insecure. He offered to take care of me, love me forever, and never let anyone hurt me. I wish I would have known that he really meant never let anyone other than "him."

Whenever we were in public, he would insist I never leave his side, or would chain his dog to a pole and make me stay next to it to keep me "safe." He would go on for hours talking about how he had affiliations with the mob and how he was an independent biker who never joined a club, as he needed to stay invisible to the police.

The stories of his life were fascinating to me, and I believed them all. I was raised in a huge Italian extended family and the day I left home was the day I ceased being a part of it. We married, moved far away, and I was alone. He would profess his love, and tell me that he was the only person who truly cared for me. Anytime we would make a friend, he would eventually have an argument with them and it would be over. I was in therapy twice a week for my bulimia, but he insisted I was having an affair with the therapist, so that ended.

After our fourth child was born he insisted that if I truly loved him and wanted him to be happy, I would have sex with a friend of his. I resisted for what seemed an eternity. After months of continued torture of sleep deprivation, silent treatments, rage, etc., I gave in. It continued for a long time, and he would eventually participate instead of just watching. I reached a point where I could no longer handle the pain.

I tried to take my life several times, but in my heart I knew I couldn't leave my precious children with the monster. Whenever I would cry out to him about what I could not bear, he would tell me that I was just being selfish, silly, or stupid. Eventually we had three more children, he became morbidly obese and was on oxygen, and the children and I waited on him hand and foot, as he was in a wheelchair.

For years I totally devoted myself to his care. I developed fibromyalgia, depression and migraines. The only help or interactions we had were with members of our church. When we moved to a small town, I started a dog rescue. With the help of other like-minded, strong, loving women, I started to see myself in the companion animals that I saved from death. As my rescue became more well known, he became more angry and defensive. He would complain endlessly that I spent too much time on my computer and even had my son look through it, as he was convinced that I was having an affair with a childhood friend. He even copied messages and sent them to my adult children as "proof."

As incidents escalated, I was becoming increasingly aware that his behavior was dangerous. Behind my back he was trying to destroy me and have our three minor children taken away and put into foster care. When he would drive me to the point of rage, he called me crazy and unstable, claiming that was all he needed to prove that I was not a fit mother.

He even moved outside into his old fifteen-passenger van with his dog because he couldn't be in the same house as a "lying, cheating whore." That was his catch phrase for me. Then a wonderful woman who became a loving friend recognized my pain and offered my children—two- and four-legged—and I sanctuary.

I learned that his plans to destroy me were not just threats, but very real, so the children and I made a plan to escape. Whenever he would leave the house, we would pack things that were needed, such as valuable paperwork, clothes, etc., into the trunk of the car that my friend had given me. After weeks of sorting through valuables, we made a date for our exodus. Before we left I went to court and obtained an order of protection against him. The car was packed and we were ready. The look on his face as I drove up to the house with the police was priceless. Of course, he had to tell the officer that I was "a lying, cheating whore who was addicted to and having sex for drugs."

It was hard. I was slandered to the point of almost losing my sanity. The stories and rumors he created were awful. I was able to get a two-year order of protection and my sister is paying for my divorce. We left that day, and have not looked back. He tells everyone he has been abused by me and that I am going to be destroyed when he tells his story. He even contested the divorce, although he wanted to be rid of me.

We are out of the state now. I will not say that it has been easy. Each day has its own challenge, as my captivity was thirty years. If it wasn't for the love of others, I can't say that I would have ever had a chance to be free. I do know that I will NEVER be silent or go back to that awful existence. We are surrounded by love and have been going to family counseling. Not all of my adult children believe me and some think that I'm "lying and overreacting." I hid my abuse well, until the end, but now, I am breaking that silence.

I want my legacy to my children to be one of empowerment and life. I will continue to speak out for and help other women who are in crisis. We all need to lean on and lift each other up. I was very fortunate to have somewhere to run. I pray for those who are still struggling to find freedom. My advice is to take their threats seriously. Make a plan, speak out, and run, never looking back.

If I found my voice after thirty years, so can you.

—Alaina Hatfield

SEVEN YEARS AGO

SEVEN YEARS AGO I MADE an incredible, life-changing decision to leave my toxic and violent marriage. The emotional, psychological and financial abuse that I had suffered through for years had reached unimaginable levels, to the point that one day I found myself in an emergency ward with doctors hovering over me, fearing that I'd had a stroke.

I could no longer speak. Nor did I want to.

Narcissistic abuse had finally tightened that grasp that it held on me to the point that my brain was signaling to me that I no longer wanted to be alive. I didn't want to live for anyone or any reason: Not for me, not for my children, not for my family or friends who loved me so much, not for anyone.

Despite reaching that low point, I was genuinely convinced that I was clinically insane and that my estranged husband was right. It was me who was mad, me who was dumb, me who was nasty, me who was ugly, me who wasn't supportive.

The list of projective language that he used against was infinite, and he abused me with that language on a daily basis. For over twenty years I heard the phrases, "You are," "You did," "You can't." Those were ones that became easy to bear.

There are two phrases that have never left the recesses of my memory. The first is, "Your tears are a weapon," which he always said as I inevitably ended up crying as a result of his abuse and accusatory outbursts during which he'd fault me for his mistakes. The second is, "You never support me." He said those words when I resigned as a Director from our jointly owned company after twelve years to accept a position in media after studying journalism.

I had finally realized that in the world outside of my front door I wasn't seen as dumb, ugly or unsupportive. In fact, the truth was quite the opposite. I had gained distinctions and very encouraging, worthy feedback in my study. I had realized that I wasn't unattractive and that my family and friends loved me for my loyalty, caring and kindness.

Despite these revelations, the three-letter word "why" consumed my everyday thinking. Why did the man who told me that he loved me treat me with such disdain? Why did he constantly put me in a dark place? Why did he make me cry every night? Why did he show me such disrespect? Why was he not proud of me? Why did he treat our three children with anger and resentment, especially our only son? Why? Why? Why? These questions eventually led me to be hospitalized, unable to speak and wanting to die.

Upon being examined by the head of psychiatry, it was explained to my parents and brother that I was a victim of serious psychological abuse. I attended extensive therapy where I learned about narcissism, a personality disorder that caused almost irreparable damage to victims.

After twenty years of various and vicious attacks, including being threatened with a 308 rifle, him threatening suicide on several occasions if I left and always being wrong and blamed for his choices, I decided that I needed to escape. I also suffered sexual assault that he justified because I was married to him. That is a pain that I can't even begin to put into words, even now.

On the day that I told him I was leaving, he became physical and threw me against the corner of my dressing table. This act of violence damaged my back and to this day I have two herniated discs and a trapped nerve as a result. He also threw a metal basket filled with steel-cap boots at my head, which narrowly missed me, but that was thrown with such force that it went through the window behind me. I had rung my mum to tell her that he was going to kill me and had her on speakerphone so that she could hear what was happening. Imagine sitting helplessly by as your daughter begged for her mercy.

My whole life flashed before my eyes. He knew he was in trouble when I told him that the police were on their way, so he jumped in his car and left. I hung up on my mum and rang the police, who turned up moments later. They examined my room where the attack took place and asked me to make a statement and get medical attention.

The next three years resulted in crippling physical, mental and emotional pain. He was brought up on aggravated assault charges, and our case was assigned to the federal family court, which caused immense, if not worse abuse, than I had suffered previously. His allegations, lies and horrific letters from his legal counsel numbed every part of me.

One day, I was taken to a coffee shop by the police prosecutor, who strongly advised me to withdraw my statement and thereby the charges, as he had hired a top barrister who would get him off of the charges.

I was living a nightmare of extremes and as my belief that the police and prosecutors were there to help and protect me unraveled before my eyes, I felt myself slipping into a state of extreme denial and fear. Ultimately I lost everything that I had worked throughout my life except for my pulse.

It is seven years now since the day that I began my journey to healing. I am living in poverty, left with emotional and psychological injuries that I will never heal from, a back injury requiring surgery, and no credit rating.

Due to him being on household accounts that he didn't pay on, our gas, electricity, water, phone and Internet were shut off, leaving me and our children destitute in our own home with no way to restore the amenities. I couldn't pay the bills because despite having joint bank accounts, the bills were only in his name, so I couldn't access them due to privacy laws.

He abused me on a daily basis, and then it felt as though the system was punishing me as well. It became impossible to work, as my health continued to deteriorate. The intense stress that I felt for all of those years resulted in a stress-related and permanent condition where there are no functioning stress hormones left in my body.

So I exist in a land of struggle and strife. Forgotten. Unheard. Abandoned. Injured. Broke. Damaged. These are all systemic results that are commonly seen in victims of domestic and psychological violence.

Despite these difficult circumstances, I feel blessed to have escaped the abuse of that terrible man with my life.

And that is saying much, much more than I could seven years ago.

—*E. J. Mason*

SLAY THE DRAGON

AFTER ATTEMPTING TO MURDER ME, sending a cartel member to kill me, beating me beyond recognition, and forcing me into witness relocation, my first narcissist was the boogieman under my bed.

A 24-hour incident of kidnapping, rape, and attempted murder proved the most terrifying thing I had ever been through. This string of violent events that nearly killed me landed my narcissist in a federal prison for seven years following our six-month relationship. Unfortunately, his incarceration didn't stop his threatening phone calls to my private federal line or his loyal affiliates from busting guns through my windows.

The horrible nightmares and memories of his terrifying rants, daily interrogation, and abuse, including his coup de grâce—the brutal finale of violence that nearly resulted in my death—were beyond comprehension.

Entering Witness Relocation, I was isolated and running scared. It seemed there was no end to the madness in sight. Painfully alone, I turned to the computer for companionship and thought my luck changed. The Internet sent me my second narcissist, with flowers and candy in hand. The minute I saw him and we locked eyes I was "saved." My damaged body, heart, and mind were so exhausted from the violence and the brutal existence I'd endured that when he came into my life, I felt like I could breathe for the first time. Finally!

My Superman had come to save the day. Because of this, and until my discard eight years later, I would tell him every day that he was the only person I had ever "loved and trusted" and that he was my "very favorite person in the entire world." I meant those words from the bottom of my heart. When I told him this every day, he would always smile and say, "I know."

A romantic, handsome, charming man, my second narcissist in the beginning seemed to be my savior, but in the end was the cause of my near emotional demise. He put me on the highest pedestal and made me his queen. He told the entire world that I was his and that no one would hurt me again. He took my drained, damaged soul and "repaired " it, healing every wound in my heart that my first narcissist had inflicted with not only with his knife and fists, but with this cruel words as well.

I never would have guessed that my second narcissist, my superhero, would be more deadly than my first without even laying a hand on me. When we first met, he promised me that he would never leave. Like all narcissists, he promised many things. Our first several years were a whirlwind of romance. He was a successful accountant, an intellect, and the sweetest, kindest man I'd ever met. I told him the entire horrible story of abuse and the final attempt on my life. Rather than judging or pushing me away for being too damaged, he embraced me and made me feel loved and accepted.

Things were wonderful for about three months, then his mask started to slip. That's when the subtle insults and head games began. First they were about my weight. I'd struggled with an eating disorder my whole life and was incredibly sensitive to criticism regarding it. He had always seemed to respect this. One day at breakfast he suggested that maybe I should cut down on my intake, as I was getting a little "pudgy." My violent bout with my first narcissist had left me barely surviving at 80 pounds. I was at 110 pounds when my second narcissist hinted that I should lose weight. As I look back, I was in no way "pudgy."

His insults started getting a bit more blatant. Soon it seemed as though I couldn't do anything right. Dinner was never hot enough, the house was never clean enough and my friends, as he'd pointed out, were all "losers." It seemed as if it was always he and I against the world. Now I can see how blinded I was to my growing isolation and the gradual loss of what little sense of self remained. The chipping away of my personality and self-esteem soon followed.

My second narcissist was an intellect and often questioned condescendingly if I was "serious" when I didn't understand something he's said or asked him to explain. I began not only questioning my intelligence, but by the end of our relationship, my reason for existence. His gaslighting and twisted recollection of events during an average discussion had me convinced that I was losing my mind and needed serious help. He finally suggested that I see a therapist and begin medication to fix my failing memory.

The brutal beating I had taken from my previous narcissist years earlier had seriously affected my memory and it seemed as though it was escaping me all over again. I couldn't remember any event correctly and was often corrected, accused of recalling the events in the wrong order or "fabricating" stories to occur as I'd wished they would have, especially if he was to blame in any way.

I'd also started misplacing things and losing items after just having had them in my hand. This was incredibly disturbing. I began seriously questioning not only the reliability of my memory, but my sanity as well. I even went so far as to check myself into a hospital for memory testing, hoping that my neurologist could find the source of my occasional amnesia and constant twisting of events. I remember wondering if there was any chance that my narcissist and his controlling behavior were the cause of these bouts of forgetfulness and mysterious movements of objects.

Next came the accusations about my fidelity. He accused me of cheating, despite the fact that during the last two years of our relationship, I was not allowed to go to his house where he and his very handsome three roommates lived. He lived in a beach house in an upscale community where his roommates often had girls running half-naked from room to room and parties nearly every day.

During the final years of our relationship, he wouldn't even be seen with me in public, claiming that I embarrassed him with my weight issues. He said I couldn't be counted on to look decent at any event. I once cornered him into taking me to his house for a weekend. During an evening of our visit, as I excitedly chattered to his roommates, behind my back he was making "pig" faces and laughing at my expense. This devaluation was incredibly painful and it quickly led to my brutal discard, the humiliation of which was nearly unbearable coming from my hero and the very love of my life.

By the end, I was convinced that I was repulsive and awkward, deserving the terrible treatment I was enduring. My self-esteem was at an all-time low and I was writhing in self-hatred. I had gone from perfection to a piece of trash and he let me know every day how he felt about me with his growing contempt and rage.

One day during a "silent treatment" episode, I was reading an article about narcissism. As my eyes scanned the page I could not believe how much he fit the criteria. I purchased an online book on the topic and quickly ingested its contents with growing dread. Could my hero be this horrible monster? It seemed nothing I did was good enough and according to him, I was a pathetic excuse for a partner whom he was staying with because he felt too "bad" to leave.

After two years of not being "allowed' to go to his house, it is hard to tell at what point in the discard I was replaced. I trusted him with every fiber of my being. Not only was he my boyfriend of eight years, but after everything that had happened with my health after my first narcissist, I'd also made him my legal guardian and overseer of my finances. He dispersed my money to me in an "allowance" once a week, an arrangement that was necessary according to him because of my "failing memory" and inability to manage money.

Suddenly my finances just weren't adding up. When I questioned him several times regarding this, he told me I miscounted, criticizing me for not saving grocery receipts, and accused me of being "incompetent" at math. When I continued to press the issue his insistence soon became rage and he screamed, "Do you think I of all people would steal from you?" Would he? With my failing health, I had become dependent on Disability and Social Security and since he was a successful banker, surely I was mistaken about the missing money.

His loss of interest in sex, romantic regress, reluctance to spend time together, and all-around distaste for me was evident at the end of my discard. Since he was my "legal guardian, lover, father, best friend, mentor, savior and ultimate hero," my life slowly meant less and less to me and the sadness in the abyss of my heart grew deeper. Finally the inevitable happened and he dumped me.

After eight years of painful putdowns, his laughing in my face as I cried, insistence that the only thing I'd been good for was giving him great oral sex and being a wonderful "whore" in the bedroom and constant chipping away at my self esteem, we were through. How could someone I loved so very much have become so cruel? He stated that all my issues had "worn him out." Two months after our breakup, he started dating a beautiful woman and began talking about marriage. In our eight years together he would not even live with me, yet after two months with the new woman in his life, he was talking about them buying a house and getting married.

Only later did I figure out that this woman had been the object of his infidelity. As it is with all narcissists, he'd secured her as his new "supply" before discarding the one he'd used up and destroyed: me. I felt empty, drained and destroyed, all because I loved someone with my entire heart. My hero, the man who saved me, had become the real monster himself.

After reading numerous books on narcissism, joining several forums and groups dedicated to the healing of victims of narcissism and counseling with a trauma therapist, I'm alone. As depressing as it sometimes feels, I notice that in the early morning, right before I am fully awake, there is a moment of peace that was not there before.

I am much more gentle with myself. I try to see the beauty in the little things, including myself. I remind myself that although my handsome knight turned out to be a dragon, I slayed the dragon and won ... and somehow ... without that knight ... I get by.

—*Rebecca McGranahan*

IF I JUST ...

"IF I JUST ..." SOUND familiar? That's a thought I remember having often. All I wanted was for us to have a good life, a healthy relationship and a good or at least manageable future. Things were falling apart and I was desperately trying to keep them from falling, every day, more than I ever concentrated on my own things.

There was worry about him passing his courses, getting him to apply for summer jobs (which even according to his grandparents became my responsibility), writing a CV, getting him to take care of his finances that directly influenced ours (or when he invested his money on gold bricks and old computer parts that laid around our apartment and aggravated my asthma), taking care of our home and previously his mom's (where cooking pots were dished and stored in the bathtub), his refusal to deal with his drinking problems, our relationship, the way he treated me and so on. If here and now did not work, then what would our future look like? I had a long time ago accepted this was it, my future was with him. I guess you could say that I became a single parent at seventeen.

So many times I wished that he would have cared enough to take care of himself, so that I didn't have to. That he would have cared about me? Or us? If I just fixed this thing. If I just learned to take care of him. If I just kept reminding him. If I just would beg him to stop and tell him how it hurts. If I just would tell him about my worries. If I just showed him enough love, maybe he would change.

Would I get to do those things I wanted, in five years, or maybe in ten ... or ever? If I just cut down on my own dreams, then maybe, just maybe, I'd have time just for one? As the years went by, I forgot myself.

Don't ever put your own needs and dreams aside, life's too short and it's your life, too! And learn this: it's not your responsibility to fix someone else; they should be strong enough to face themselves and mature enough to build themselves for the better.

After an experience like this, we may feel like we're not capable, that our spark for trying has been worn out. But what if we looked at that energy we had, that energy we had to just try. We did it for love, right? Because we believed in it and hopefully still do. Love isn't something that you just find in relationships. It's something you can feel for your own well-being too.

So what if ... I just ... breathe? What If I just ... spoke kindly to myself? What If I just ... listened to my own needs? It takes time and it isn't all that easy.

But what if this time we'll change that sentence, change that hopeless "if" and "just" and say, "This time—I'll be here for me."

—Emilia Strong

THE DARK CARNIVAL

FOR 2½ YEARS, I WAS with a man I deeply loved, and lived part-time with in Seattle. I traveled back and forth between there and an outlying town, where I need to stay for my dogs, of whom I share custody with my ex-husband. Sadly, now I'm in mourning for the end of that life, due to the recent revelation that my partner was not who he appeared to be, or said he was; he had a whole dark carnival of secrets and lies going on in his head, which I only found out about after inadvertently kicking over a rock in his internet life, and being stunned by what crawled out from under it.

In the ensuing time, I've gotten enough distance from him to see the patterns of emotional abuse that led up to this. A graphic created by Leslie Vernick of Emotionally Abusive Behaviors & Attitudes was especially edifying to come across because I realized I had no problem easily citing examples of every one of the things listed.

I feel compelled now to warn others about the signs of these toxic situations. If you recognize any of the behaviors and attitudes listed below being directed at you by anyone close, please grab your dignity and get the hell out; there's no winning with these spiritual defectives, and it will only get worse.

- Withholding
- Restricting
- Isolating
- Threatening
- Abandoning
- Raging
- Constant Criticism
- Ridiculing
- Demeaning
- Belittling
- Coercing

- Accusing
- Ordering
- Ignoring
- Minimizing
- Subtle nonverbal cues
- Denying one's reality
- Negative labeling
- Chronic deceit

Some of these people, as I've come to learn, have narcissistic personality disorder (NPD), as I believe my former partner does. Of course, I am not a doctor qualified to diagnose someone, but article after article on NPD described the agony of my experience in shockingly familiar detail so, if the shoe fits, better safe than sorry, run from it. Honor yourself, and unconditionally love yourself more than you love them. Survivors of this abuse know more intimately about the devastating reality and excruciating fallout of this condition than any doctor with only clinical experience of these people can comprehend.

I kept feeling that the way this man was treating me was spiritually criminal, and now I know these people are not legally insane; they are morally insane, by choice. It is hard to accept that I didn't recognize sooner what I was dealing with, but my pure heart had never encountered, let alone had my trust shattered and betrayed by, such a master manipulator before, one who never planned to be unmasked by me.

> "Through their research they gradually realize that the narcissist never really loved them or anyone for that matter, as they are wholly incapable of love and devoid of a conscience. Survivors reluctantly come to accept that the person they were in love with was just a cleverly crafted façade that never really existed. Finally, this realization forces them to mourn the loss of two people only amplifying and adding to their grief. First, they must mourn the loss of the person they loved who never really existed and second, they must mourn the loss of person they believed their narcissist had the potential to be."
>
> —Bree Bonchay, LCSW, http://relationshipedia.me

In actuality, he was a pathologically selfish, sucking black hole of endless, restless need and lack of reciprocity, which I've come to know is a called a "narcopath"—or person with NPD. Finding websites and forums, like Bree Bonchay's, above, and Richard Gannon's Spartan Life Coach channel on YouTube, among others, have helped me immensely in recovering from what has been the most painful, disturbing. and baffling relationship of my life. I've learned much about what I am seeking in a partner by all the ways he was lacking, as well as reclaimed my own sense of self-worth and spiritual sovereignty.

Six months have passed now, and the more I research this subject and talk to other survivors, the more shocked I am that I never knew about this before. I'm dismayed by the pervasiveness, and everybody should know the signs. One of these predators will never make it past my gate again; as one fellow survivor put it in an online forum I like: now, I can see the red flags from space!

I've been reading everything I can find from my local library, and recently had a book out called *Freeing Yourself from the Narcissist in Your Life*, by Linda Martinez-Lewi, PhD. The very next time I went to the library to pick up something on the holds shelf, the familiar cover caught my eye of that same book, in the slot next to mine, for someone whose name started with the next letter over. I felt so sad for the person who also was going through the same thing, but what are the odds of two people next to each other alphabetically on a library holds shelf in a small city having need of that book at the same time? How many other copies were under the other letters on that day?

This is clearly some kind of epidemic, a modern-day plague. There is fascinating evidence cited in books such as *Evil Genes: Why Rome Fell, Hitler Rose, Enron Failed, and My Sister Stole My Mother's Boyfriend* by Barbara Oakley, about brain research on these folks, and they have notable differences in brain structure in the areas where fight or flight impulses originate, and another abnormality where empathy lives in the rest of us. Part of the reason for the growing awareness of what a scourge these Cluster B defects (narcissistic, borderline, antisocial and histrionic personality disorders) are is the sheer numbers of the afflicted. It seems disproportionately high possibly because narcissists tend to have more sex than other people due to their inflated opinion of their own desirability, extremely fluid boundaries, and that they seem to love to see themselves in their mini-me's—what a favor they believe they are doing the world to leave more just like themselves behind!

Oakley also describes studies of an Eskimo tribe and an African tribe that each had a word in their languages for the personality-disordered, and tellingly, in both cultures the medicine men and women considered the glitch incurable. She asked the Eskimo what the tribe would do about them, and he said, ideally, one of them would get him alone on an ice floe and shove him off. Sounds like justice to me!

It is chilling for me to realize how lucky I was to see the abuser "unmasked" before I invested even more time and wasted even more love on him, since he so convincingly played the Love of My Life. I'll never forget the way he behaved before he knew what I knew about him, as I, a classically trained, professional actress, could only marvel in speechless horror at a performance straight out of the Ted Bundy School of Acting. What was under his mask was no woman's idea of blissful partnership material. I dodged a soul bullet.

—*Chantal Cayce*

REFLECTIONS

I WAS ONCE IN AN abusive relationship.

It started out simple enough: a chance meeting on a dating site, a long conversation, and a promise to meet. I thought that he seemed nice, if a tad emotional (he cries easily). Later on I realized that his tears were a warning sign.

I was young and naïve. I'd only dated a few men before, and while they had all been nice, it never worked out.

The first time we met, he took me for a drive and a long walk along the coast. We spoke about our pasts, our expectations, and whatever else came up. It was a good day. We got to know each other, and I believed he was a great guy. At 50, he had never been in a relationship, which I found strange, but didn't question much. Had I, I would've kept my eye out for more warning signs.

We met again the very next day. We again went for a drive, and I told him about my dietary choices (I don't eat chicken and beef). Most people are curious as to why and question me, but always respect my decision. He, however, told me that I was being silly and vowed to change me. There was something in his tone that made me a little uncomfortable, but I pushed it aside, believing he was probably joking.

Later that day, back at my place, we spent the evening cuddling on my bed. Then he said something shocking.

"I love you," he said.

I was stunned. I had only known him two days and he was saying he loved me? He hardly knew me. I personally felt little for him. Attraction, perhaps, but not love. I thanked him for his admission, and said that while I respected his feelings, I couldn't reciprocate, because it was too soon.

What happened next was like something out of a movie. He ran out of my room crying. I tried running after him to calm him, but tears were streaming down his face while he got into his car and ignored me.

"I don't know if I want to see you again," he said before driving away, leaving me standing there feeling terrible for hurting him. Later on, I realized that this was one of his ways to assume control over me—emotionally blackmailing me through guilt so that I would give into his demands.

I spent the next two days apologizing via text, feeling increasingly bad about it because he refused to accept my apology. He told me that I was making excuses for not caring about how he felt. Nothing I said was enough, and he was punishing me for rejecting him. It made him feel powerful, and he wielded that power with impunity.

When we met again, I invited him over. We were sitting on the bed, and I was telling him about my day. He looked at me and said, "Shut up. You talk too much."

I'm not normally someone who talks a lot, nor am I someone who accepts rudeness. But because of all the past confusion and emotional blackmail, I apologized and stopped talking. It was one of the most disempowering moments I had ever experienced; he was literally telling me that I didn't matter. This continued over our next few dates with no sign of abating. I liked him, but it was starting to hurt too much.

I felt like I had to get away, so I took a trip to visit friends. As soon as I arrived, I breathed a great sigh of relief. It felt like a huge burden had been lifted off my shoulders, knowing I was away from him and his manipulations for a few days.

Sadly, it was too good to be true. He started messaging me, telling me how terrible and cruel I was for leaving him alone, how heartless I was for not being there with him, how lonely he felt without me. This continued and I did my best to put him out of my mind, but he would then put up a wall of silence when I tried asking him about his day. He had no interest in what I was doing, or the friends I was meeting; they were all nonsense compared to his own feelings.

When I returned, we met up again. He was going to be taking photographs at a race, and asked me to come with him, saying we would pick up lunch along the way. He took me to KFC. I didn't eat chicken and he brought me to a place that served nothing but.

Thinking it was an innocent mistake, I pointed it out to him. He claimed he had forgotten, and there was no time to go elsewhere. He bought me a small pack of chips while he ate a wrap. I realized then that he was serious about trying to change me. At that point, I was already so weakened by the unequal power dynamics that I went along without complaining.

He had succeeded. He had changed me. I was no longer my own man, but merely a body for his amusement. My feelings didn't matter; only his did. My friends didn't matter; only he did. My preferences didn't matter; only what he dictated did. I was broken after weeks of emotional manipulation, blackmail and control.

That was the last time I saw him.

No, he did not die. He's probably still out there, torturing whoever he is dating.

I finally decided I was tired of him. I didn't want to feel the way I did anymore. At that point, I still had not realized that he was being abusive. I just thought that we were too different and I told him that. He railed. He guilted. He made promises. He begged. But I was firm.

That very day, I moved into a friend's place so he couldn't find me. I was actually hiding because I didn't want him to come to my place and convince me to return to him. I was afraid that he would succeed. Given my emotional state at the time, he may have, had it not been for my friend, who stood by me and helped me through the whole experience.

Over the next few months, as I slowly regained my self-esteem and became emotionally stable, I started analyzing his actions and realized that they were all done with horrifying preciseness and calculation.

He was breaking me down with his words, slowly; gradually, until I could no longer defy him. Until I was nothing but a puppet doing his bidding.

He never hit me or threatened to hit me. What he did was worse; it was subtle, so you don't realize it until it's too late for you to escape. He disguised it with kindness and love, pretty words that served to lower your defenses, allowing him to hit you at your weakest point. He knew exactly what he was doing and that was the most terrifying thing.

To this day, I am incredibly thankful that I escaped. I have lost my innocence and been exposed to the ugliness of the world. While that is regrettable, it is okay because I know what an abusive relationship is like and what the warning signs are.

I know what to do if I find myself in one again, and I can use this experience to help others who may find themselves in the same situation.

There is no one obvious sign for abuse. In fact, the person dispensing it will be careful not to let you realize that he or she is abusing you.

They will dress their actions in loving words.

They will do it slowly and subtly, so you do not realize what is happening.

With guarded patience, they will try and assume control over your actions and feelings, and finally, they will turn your own thoughts against you, so you will be abusing yourself.

If you find yourself in such a situation, stop and question it. Move away from the abuser and spend time with a neutral third party who can help you unpack your emotions and understand what has been done to you.

It will be difficult: the abuser will do everything he can to stop you, and you must be strong enough to resist him. It will be painful: you will realize how terribly you have been treated by someone you thought cared about you, and it will hurt like hell. It will feel like you cannot ever trust another person again: that is okay. You have faced a traumatizing situation and you need time to overcome it.

I promise you that one day, it will get better. It will be possible to trust and love again, and I know that for a fact because I have done that. I have emerged stronger than ever from the abuse, and because of that, I value the experience.

I have no idea where I found the strength to walk away, but I now know that it is inside me, ready to come out when necessary. I know I am not weak; in fact, I'm far from it. I have survived an abusive relationship, and it has helped shape who am I today.

For that, I am grateful.

—*Ng Jern Siong*

CHAPTER 3

PAINFUL LESSONS

The lessons we learn from pain will always make us the strongest.
—Anonymous

LETTER TO MY NARCISSIST

THIS IS A LETTER TO my narcissist. I'm not sure if I'm supposed to write this as if you are a human being, or as if you are what I know you are now.

Because I didn't know what you were. I didn't understand that you feigned human emotions. I didn't realize it was all a beautifully orchestrated, choreographed manipulation from the very first day.

I was made for you; you said it so many times and you were right, my narcissistic lover—I was made for your abuse, and you knew it on a level I couldn't possibly understand. You targeted me and I unwittingly and unknowingly invited you in like a hapless victim invites a vampire across their threshold. I welcomed your "love" with open arms and a pure heart, and you fed off my emotions; an emotional vampire, you took advantage of my vulnerability, manipulated me, used me at every turn and I was so brainwashed that I believed it was love.

I remember our first conversation. Everything I said, you mimicked. What a miracle it was to find a person who felt the same as I did. You were the finest actor. God, how you wanted me. That feeling of being the center of your world was unlike anything I have ever felt before or will ever feel again. You set your sights on me and you were going to stop at nothing until you had me. I know now that you were motivated by the thrill of the chase. That you had kicked full throttle into the first phase of narcissistic abuse: the Idealization phase.

Remember all the things you said to me? Those months when you had me on that pedestal, so precariously balanced on that pedestal. The lavish gifts, that weekend where you spared no expense; how you told me that I was "the one that God designed exactly for you." I believed you. I soaked it up like sunshine. I remember being the focus of your laser attention and the gravity that your world depended upon, and it was unlike anything I had ever felt in my life.

I loved you. I loved the illusion you presented. I loved that person you were in the beginning, that false self, that man that you worked so hard to convince me that you were. That man that promised me the world. That man who promised me he would never hurt me.

All those nights I cried and I shared with you my hurt and my vulnerability, you soaked it up and filed it away just to use against me in the Devaluation phase. You used my trust in you against me. I hate you, the vindictive and petty and narcissistic you, the fearful and treacherous you, the void and unreal you, the person underneath the mask you pretended to be to lure me into your web of deceit. The hardest thing for me to accept is that the person who I thought you were, the person who claimed to love me, never existed.

Slowly and insidiously over time you criticized every single part of my self-confidence and self-worth. Everything about me was wrong. I absorbed it all and I began to see myself through your dark and twisted eyes. I was no longer the confident and secure woman that I was before you came into my life. You drained my self-esteem and replaced it with anxiety and insecurity. I felt I could never do anything right. You were always angry, a deep and simmering anger beneath the surface. I was walking on eggshells every second of my life, never knowing what I might say or do next to set you off.

It was your use of the silent treatment and withdrawal that was the most damaging and harmful to me. I think about the hundreds of times over four years that you iced me out, shut me out, ignored me, refused to speak to me, wouldn't acknowledge my presence, wouldn't acknowledge or answer my emails or texts, would refuse my phone calls, and wouldn't even LOOK at me when we lived in the same house.

You are a master at being the silent abuser, and you are in denial over your own abuse.

The silent treatment is the worst form of emotional abuse. It is a punishment used by abusers to make you feel unimportant, unvalued, uncared about and completely absent from the abuser's thoughts. It is used as a form of non-physical punishment and control because the abuser mistakenly thinks that if they don't physically harm you, then they are not abusers. The truth is they are far worse at doling out abuse than the physical abuser. In a sense you have been psychologically murdered by them, but your physical life goes on.

The hardest part of all of this is having to accept that the person who I thought you were never existed. It was the mask, the mirroring, the love-bombing, the fake promises and the ILLUSION that you presented to me that I believed I loved. The real you is all that came afterwards: the selfish, controlling, manipulative and emotionally abusive person who lied and punished me mercilessly for every bit of narcissistic injury you experienced and blamed me for, the person who projected every ounce of narcissistic rage upon me, the person who hurt me and abandoned me emotionally and physically over and over and over again until you abandoned me for the final time.

Thank you for leaving. It saved my life.

I am going to get healthy now. I am going to heal my inner wounds, the ones that led me to you, the ones that made me vulnerable to you and your manipulation. I am going to learn my value, and understand my worth, and know what my boundaries are, and take care of ME, treat myself kindly, with respect and love.

I am going to invite love and happiness and create peace and sanity in my world. I don't know that I would have ever truly understood how codependent I am, how my codependency led me down the wrong road over and over again, how I confused love with abuse, how I spent years of my life loving people who could never love me in return, who could never give me what I needed or wanted or deserved, because I couldn't give me what I needed, wanted or deserved.

I knew I had something to learn from you and as painful as this experience has been, I learned the most important lesson of my entire life.

I learned that I deserve real love.

I learned that I chose my own destruction.

I learned that I can change this dysfunctional pattern, that I have the power, that I can choose to be happy and healthy, and that I am no longer going to stumble though my life in the dark, allowing my pain and my subconscious wounds to take the lead and make the decisions.

I am awake. And for that I will always be grateful.

—Hope Jay

COVERT NARCISSISM

The parable and metaphor goes as this: if you drop a frog in a pot of boiling water, it will of course frantically try to clamber out. But if you place it gently in a pot of tepid water and turn the heat on low, it will float there quite placidly. As the water gradually heats up, the frog will sink into a tranquil stupor, exactly like one of us in a hot bath, and before long, with a smile on its face, will unresistingly allow itself to be boiled to death.

(—Daniel Quinn, *The Story of B*)

I STAND BEFORE YOU AS a 58-year-old woman. A woman who has training and credentials—a counseling degree, massage therapy certification and a nursing license. A woman benefitting from the life experiences of being a divorced, single mother and an adult survivor of childhood sexual abuse and violence. A woman who has traversed so many pitfalls of bad relationships, poverty, and trauma that you would think I'd known better. After decades of walking the tightrope, often caught between hanging on and losing it, I thought I'd been exposed to nearly every kind of situation and considered myself quite savvy.

But I wasn't savvy enough, nor did I know better. I've scolded myself repeatedly that I should have recognized the signs of abuse as they reared their ugly heads again. I fell into the abyss again not from lack of experience, knowledge or from lack of therapeutic work. I was a 20-plus-year veteran of therapy, had logged decades in Al-Anon, practiced alternative healing modalities. Yet, I fell prey to a narcissistic Christian family who fooled me completely from the very beginning because their narcissism was covert.

I've had months to reflect on my situation since I've been released from my third in-patient hospitalization for attempting suicide. The therapists in my life, inpatient and otherwise, have pressed me hard to identify the triggers of my latest attempts to end my life. We've methodically dissected these events in an effort to look at them and the pain they've caused. We've broken them apart to begin the process of rebuilding. It's been an arduous challenge, one that I didn't even want to start. I fought hard against the raging demons in my head that told me that I was too old, too stupid, too broken to begin again. If it wasn't for the terror in my daughter's eyes as she looked at my arms that I'd cut and slashed, I probably wouldn't have. I'd failed her again and owed her another try.

During the last six months, I've been painfully alone and isolated. My husband, one of my narcissists, left me and our marriage, taking his entire family with him, along with his own version of a total meltdown and identity crisis. In one fell swoop, he changed his mind about wanting to be married, cut ties from our daughter, listed our home for sale and decided he needed to quit his job.

From the moment he left, I became invisible to him and his family. Almost overnight, my identity changed. I was no longer their beloved daughter-in-law, I no longer had his two sisters as friends, their children ceased to be my daughter's cousins, our church sided with their esteemed ex-minister and leader, my father-in-law. My phone calls went unreturned. Birthdays, holidays, weddings came and went without a word from them. All the benefits and safety of being within a family dissipated and I was left reeling from the sudden, profound loss. It was like losing my entire family, from the elders to the great-grand-babies, in one moment.

My husband's inability to fight the controlling, narcissistic dynamics in his own family prompted this action. Up until now and during the twelve years of our marriage, he had found my fiery and honest nature appealing. I served as a lifeline to the side of him that internally rejected his family's pathology. I was the free spirit, loving and listening with an open heart, giving myself completely to him as he'd never previously experienced from his cold and unfeeling parents. But as time went on and I continued to stand up to his controlling patriarch of a father, I eventually became the pariah that needed to be disposed of. When he finally gave up the fight, surrendering to his prescribed role, I no longer fit. I had served my purpose.

My father-in-law is a Methodist bishop and minister. On the surface, he is a highly educated man holding a PhD, and is a well-respected member in his arena of religious leaders and community. He rose through the ranks from a small-town minister to a powerful administrator of a multistate district. He isn't an alcoholic, drug addict, or sexually inappropriate in any way. He has been married to the same woman his entire life and owns a beautiful summer resort cabin where he generously entertains friends and colleagues. He's financially stable, well groomed, and eloquent. He publicly advocates for the marginalized, donates to environmental causes, embraces diversity, and champions for the underdog. Most importantly, as my therapist and I unravel the confusing mess, I've come to understand, he is also a charismatic narcissistic who managed to control and oppress his wife and three children into being the poster family for his career and image. In ways I didn't recognize because of their lack of overtness, I completely bought into the thinking and identity of this family, nearly losing my sanity and my life as a result.

My therapist and I have carefully broached the subject of red flags and warning signs. When I came to the horrible realization that they were most probably present from the beginning, it brought on an onslaught of self-flagellation. The horror of recognizing that from the onset of my relationship with my husband, the signs were indeed there was almost too much to bear. I had ignored or failed to notice them and had again put myself at risk. I had once again failed myself and my daughter. Over the weeks, we spoke gently of these warning signs—how they can be slight and tiny and covert in nature sometimes, how I came to the relationship vulnerable, how a narcissistic family, especially one sanctioned by organized religion, could be a well-oiled machine, an insidious con game that many people fail to recognize.

I still struggle to realize these truths and exhibit compassion for myself. Gradually I became able to tolerate the emotions that arose when I actually pictured myself shaking off my instincts, refusing to acknowledge the screaming voice inside of me.

Throughout most of my marriage, I thought my escalating anxiety and self-destructive behavior were a result of my childhood trauma and blamed myself for that willingly. My husband and his family were absolutely fine with my self-chastising. They approved and endorsed my methods to silence myself through multiple medications, as I willed myself mute regarding important subjects or simply was absent to their events and gatherings.

I repeatedly found myself aghast at conversations that were hollow and cold, devoid of any kind of feeling: my father-in-law turning his back on his sister during her abusive marriage and her subsequent suicide, the ostracizing of a cousin who they deemed "crazy" because she struggled with survivor guilt for living through a car crash that killed both her parents and a sister, a murder-suicide of the brother of my stepson's wife. Each of these situations, among many others, were met with merciless denial. They simply wouldn't address them, feel them, or let them tarnish their perfect image they had created. When I would try to speak of or process these events, I was shut down. Even worse, his family members would often simply refuse to speak. They remained silent through my inquiries until someone would adjourn to the kitchen for ice cream. It was only then that they became chatty and a lively conversation would ensue of how many types of toppings they would like. I know now that intuitively, I had begun to witness the one-way loyalty of a narcissist. I tried desperately to make sense of a completely distorted situation where a supposed "loved" family member was thrown under the bus. For reasons I'm still exploring and not completely sure of, I failed to recognize their insanity. Instead, I blamed myself.

That's the default mechanism that we, as survivors, often revert to. We take the most cruel and intolerable of situations and attempt to make them acceptable. Often we blame and chastise ourselves. We have to. Sometimes our lives depended on it. As the pattern became deeply rooted, our thinking became altered, deeply skewed and warped. Our instincts were in constant conflict with our survival and we were forced to adapt to survive. This is how it happened for me. My instincts about this family were overruled by my trauma and my deeply held fear that I'd never belong to a decent family. I rationalized, albeit unconsciously, that I'd be lucky to be part of this one. I lied to myself as much as the narcissist father-in-law, husband and religious family members did. I didn't have a prayer.

As I work through this last chapter, one that has reduced my coping skills to bare survival, subjected me to years of triangulation between my husband and father-in-law and robbed me of my self worth, I have recently begun to see a glimmer of hope. For during this time, I've received support and kindness from the most of unlikely people. Discovering and unfolding the concept of narcissistic abuse both online and in my therapist's office has been a lifesaver and it turns out, I'm the hero. While initially, the concept of my husband and family as narcissists seemed a far-fetched one, it has proven to have merit as I dug deeper. I can now recognize their manipulations and see their true selves as shallow and self-serving egoists. The hurt of being excluded has faded a bit. His sisters, upon closer inspection are listless and sad, something I hadn't before noticed. While they continue the charade and pathology, passing it down to their children, I realized it hasn't been an easy load to bear living a life unfulfilled in exchange for loyalty to their oppressor. They lack the ability to change, still shuffling into church on Sundays and walking blindly through their lives. In their minds, they are the ultimate Christians.

I, on the other hand, try to stay just a bit angry. It is the one emotion that continues to propel me away from not only the narcissist, but any situation that I find unhealthy. The warrior spirit serves me well. My anxiety continues to dissipate and my emotions are leveling out even though my journey isn't near finished. I still have to make big decisions: where I will live, what my future looks like, how I will care for myself, who I spend my time with. I no longer settle for being financially secure but emotionally starved. I don't have to constantly be proving my loyalty to my narcissist, frantically upping my efforts to be compliant and supportive or enduring constant disapproval for being true to myself. I breathe easier now and sleep sounder.

So, I stand here, as a 58-year-old woman, a little bit smarter, definitely more road- weary but wholly impressed with my capacity to adapt, change and learn. I've weathered another storm and am on my way to a well-earned and more complete freedom. I'd say that I have transcended, but at the very least, I've avoided being boiled to death.

—*Rescuing Little L*

BETWEEN THE LINES

WHEN I LEFT MY NARCISSIST, I knew something was wrong, but had no idea what. I was with my narcissistic husband for ten years and we had three young children. Hindsight is an amazing gift. Seeing a plan emerge from a series of supposed random events comforted me.

I learned that verbal abuse existed after I left and my relationship was nearly over. I tried explaining it to my husband, believing I had discovered the answer to our unhappiness. He ignored me and became abusive in response.

I tried desperately to save us. I told him the relationship was sinking and that I'd jumped off to save myself. I told him that if he would just take my hand, he would be saved too. I didn't realize that he was quite happy to let the ship sink since he had another one passing that he planned to board. Once he was certain that he had a new partner, he abruptly told me it was over.

Much of my time with him was spent spinning out of control. My sense of self was shaky at best. Today I am in a place of total acceptance. Before I left I was having suicidal thoughts. One dreary weekend full of arguments, moping and venomous words, I lay on the couch with my eyes shut and thought to myself, "If I was dead in a casket, it would be so peaceful and calm."

I knew I needed help.

My husband and I began taking antidepressants and started counseling. He began to collapse emotionally before my eyes, hiding in cupboards, crying, saying he couldn't work anymore. He threatened to kill himself at one point. The children heard this threat. I had no idea it was verbal abuse.

One night, my eight-year-old daughter was upset and told me that she wished she was dead. I told my husband that I was worried about the impact our arguments were having on the children.

I though we should move, and I went ahead of him, taking the children with me. When he visited on weekends, we fought constantly, often having emotional meltdowns. One day I spent over an hour at his bedside, trying to convince him to stop crying after his friend was too busy to get a beer with him.

During our relationship I had been called countless names. He used his words as weapons and it was horrendous. He tore at the very fiber of my being. He destroyed anything of any worth to me unless I did what he needed. I tried the same in retaliation.

The he last straw for me was when he called me a horrible person. I would not be around someone who believed that of me. No longer able to play the game, I checked out of the relationship.

After discovering what verbal abuse was, I thought I could save our relationship. I thought the emotional turmoil was accidental and that if we worked on it we could salvage our dream—my dream. Then I discovered something else: not only was my husband abusing me, he was unwilling to admit it, as it required something he was not prepared to give: himself.

Despite leaving, I remained open to reconciliation and therefore open to his attacks. I hadn't realized that it was hopeless. He threatened to kill himself on multiple occasions and police were involved. I took the brunt of extreme verbal abuse while being manipulated into seeing him as I tried to help him.

I was granted custody of our children as a result of his mental health. When I told his father (whom he worked for) that any day my husband could fail at work due to his mental health, his father told me his work ethic had not changed in the slightest. This confused me, and I came to realize it wasn't as much mental health as it was manipulation of me. I felt that his abuse of me needed to be addressed before he had the children unsupervised.

His mother undermined me at almost every turn, minimizing his actions and accusing me of minor offenses as though I should be studying my mistakes and brushing over his. I believed that if I spoke out and showed people what he had said and done, they would support me. In reality, not only did people turn a blind eye to protect their own perceptions, they also attacked my integrity and actions. This had a massive impact on my grasp of reality. It was hard to cling to what at times felt like only pure gut instinct. I am actually amazed at how brave and intelligent I was.

Scouring the Internet for answers, I discovered codependency, which lead me to narcissism. I could finally name things that had been plaguing me for years, the most significant being pathological loneliness, which I'd felt in my life as early as I could remember. I always wondered why I was never happy and why no matter what I had, I still felt worthless and alone.

The only thing that dimmed the feeling of worthlessness was him. The abuse seemed a happy trade. In reality, it was like a high-interest loan where I ended up paying far, far more than I could ever afford. Like any loan shark, once he saw I was defaulting on payments, he found a new client to bleed dry. When my husband realized I had nothing left to give, he took me to the cleaners. I now understood why no contact is the only way to go.

The last time I saw him, I fought with him at our old family home, while his new girlfriend was there. I was reduced to tears and left in a rage, calling out the name of a person I'd slept with in retaliation. He had me exactly where he wanted me. I begged him to come and see me before I drove home. A few days prior, he had been in my bed. Now he arrived to my parked car to tell me he absolutely did not want me as his new partner stayed back at our house. I cried for two days nonstop.

I learned that he never intended to own anything or fix anything. He sold me down the river to save himself the pain of facing his mistakes. I came to conceptualize the idea of codependency and narcissistic love: one will give the ultimate sacrifice and the other will take the ultimate price.

It is important to pay attention to the small, persistent feelings that you have when you sense that there is something amiss. As with most stories, so much is told between the lines.

—*Chloe*

THIRTEEN YEARS WITH A NARCOPATH

AS I SIT HERE FEELING the emptiness surround me, and the vacuum created by it attempts to overwhelm my soul and drag me into an endless pit filled with nothing but self-pity, I try to understand just how I got here and why.

Is this situation really all my fault, as those around me claim? Have I no one to blame but myself for the poor decision that I made in choosing a mate whose only goal was to extinguish all goodness and hope in me? To strangle any flicker of life and leave an empty shell to disintegrate into dust and blow away in a gust of wind?

Did I really ask for this, and am I now getting exactly what I deserve?

These are the thoughts rolling around in my head on any given day, at any given moment in time.

Who am I? I am a victim who is just now recovering from an attack by a narcopath (narcissistic sociopath).

It is difficult to think of oneself as a "victim," with all of the "enlightened" people out there stating with assuredness that we are all responsible for our own actions, and that we must accept responsibility for each and every choice we make. But is it really a choice when one finds oneself in the clutches of a predator? Does a deer choose to be shot by a hunter? Is that a conscious choice that should be accepted and owned?

When a narcopath hunts his prey, he deceives her into thinking that he is someone else. Someone he could never truly be. It is all a game to him, and he lays a trap so intricate and deceptive that telling it from reality is difficult at best, if not impossible.

So, I ask again, is it really a choice when you are targeted by a narcopath and fall into his snare? Does a deer choose to be targeted by the hunter and shot, or is she in the wrong place at the wrong time, having been purposely led into a carefully laid trap? And if she escapes, should she be blamed for allowing it? Is it really her fault?

For me, the game started thirteen years ago when the trap was set, and I walked into it wholly unaware of what was in store. Yes, if I had known then what I do now, I would have made a wide berth, but I didn't, and so it began.

I met whom I refer to as Tin Man, man without a heart, when I was taking care of my elderly mother. We were alone, and she was the last of my family. I am an only child. I was raised to take full responsibility for my actions, and to never give up no matter how difficult things got. I always thought that these were my strong points, but unbeknownst to me, these just happened to be the exact qualities that Tin Man was looking for, and because of them, I was lined up to be his next target.

How do you go about setting a trap to turn strengths into weaknesses in order to snare your prey? He was an expert, and did so with ease. During the course of our relationship, no matter how bad it got, he would remind me that I should never give up. No matter what hateful thing he did, he reminded me that I should bear responsibility for doing things that caused him to react the way he did. He was well-practiced at this type of manipulation, having had a previous failed 16-year relationship with someone that he constantly complained about, and repeatedly blamed for just about everything that had gone wrong in his life. In the beginning, I couldn't understand how he could stay with someone he obviously despised for 16 years, but now I realize that he was getting so much pleasure from the pain he was putting her through that he simply couldn't let go of the fix. Every time she tried to commit suicide, he must have been right there, drinking in her agony with relish.

And so I persevered. I tried to be a better person, to understand what he must have been going through, and to try and help him heal. I thought that we were building a future together. That is what he said. And I believed him. That is, until the carefully put up façade that he was hiding behind began unraveling and the true nature of the beast lurking behind the mask began surfacing more frequently until I could rationalize the behavior no more.

The road to my realization that he was not the person he appeared to be started with a lie. A simple lie, really. But a lie nonetheless. It was a lie about something that would have been better handled with the truth. So I confronted him. He looked shocked that I would even think that he would lie to me. And he said, "Do you really think I lied?" I said, "Yes." He got angry and stormed out of the room. A few days later, he started accusing me of telling people that he lies. He withdrew his attention and gave me the cold shoulder. The lying got more blatant, and the accusations got worse. Each time he lied it was even more exaggerated than the last, and I was made out to be the horrible person who lied to the neighbors by accusing him of lying. He turned it right back around and accused me of doing exactly what he was doing! And then, he would change and act like nothing had happened. I must be imagining things.

He isolated me from my friends by telling stories behind my back and then accused me of sleeping around if I talked to another man or telling stories about him if I talked to a female friend. He also made up stories about my friends, putting them in a bad light and saying how they were two-faced and how I could never trust them. He didn't want me staying at my job because of the drive in the snow and ice during winter, so I quit. And then my vehicles started mysteriously breaking down so that I couldn't get to town to get another job.

He went so far as to tell me that the neighbors hated me and were sneaking over to cut the gas lines on my truck. I use the truck to get hay for my animals, and several times while doing so, they burst and spewed gas all over the ground while I had several tons of hay in the trailer. One spark would have set me on fire. He went so far as to put a motion-activated camera under the truck at night to "catch the neighbors." No one ever came. The only person who worked on the truck was him. After he left, I never had a problem with the gas lines again after having them fixed by the neighborhood mechanic.

He would tell me how much he loved me, and in the next breath, tell me that if I wanted affection I should go stand on a street corner.

The lies were so thick and the behavior so erratic that nothing he said or did could be trusted. When we did things together he would intentionally push a little too hard, pull a little too much, until I fell or got hurt in some way and stopped wanting him to help. I learned that any interaction with him meant pain for me, and he seemed to enjoy it. He would laugh at my pain and intentionally do and say things to make it worse. We lost a goose that I raised from birth to a coyote attack. I felt badly and was crying. He told me that she committed suicide because of me.

I stopped wanting to interact with him at all. This made him angry and even more demanding because I wasn't doing enough for him.

In thirteen years, he never once celebrated my birthday. The best I got was an offhand "happy birthday" as we passed in the hallway. The last birthday I had he wanted to go online and order something for himself since I was on the computer. I refused. He got mad and accused me of not doing anything for him. The veneer was off and the true Tin Man was live and in color, and his hatred for me was apparent.

When he decided to leave, he planned to do it wreaking as much havoc as possible. My vehicles were broken down; the place was littered with garbage that he simply threw outside and left. Then he took off for California, promising to send me money for the bills and to make the house payment. For the first couple of months he allowed me to have $548 per month. This was not enough to cover the $300 electrical bill, the $585 house payment, the car insurance, phone bill, hay bill, or anything else. So, I had to make tough decisions. He told me not to pay the mortgage and he would catch things up when he got back. I didn't listen and scraped enough money together to pay it. At that point I understood that he fully intended to let me go into foreclosure after calling and promising that he would make sure that I didn't lose the house. Lies. I got food stamps, energy assistance, and got by. Then he said he needed all of the money and showed up to collect his gear and leave. I got a restraining order on him when he demanded his gun and said he hoped I would die a horrible death. I haven't seen him since, and have no idea how I will make the monthly payments. He is on his way to another victim, and I would rather be broke than be with him one more minute.

So again I ask the question that I asked in the beginning: is it really a choice when you are targeted by a narcopath and fall into his snare? Does a deer choose to be targeted by the hunter and shot, or is she in the wrong place at the wrong time, having been purposely led into a carefully laid trap? And if she escapes, should she be blamed for allowing it? Is it really her fault?

My answer? NO! It is not. If I had known then what I know now, I would have run away just as fast as I could. I would not have played the game because I would have been aware of it and headed on down the road. If you do not know that you are being deceived, it is not your fault. I do not accept the blame for being targeted by someone with no true feelings of love or remorse. It is hard to accept that some people do not think the same way as those of us who have actual feelings of love, empathy and compassion do, but they don't. They are hardwired differently for whatever reason, and they simply do not play by the rules of common decency.

I will heal eventually. He will not. He will go on to the next victim and play the same game over and over because that is the only thing that he knows how to do. He is a lost soul who doesn't know the meaning of love. Who preys on others and feeds off of their grief because that is his nature. He is not welcome here ever again. I have learned a very hard lesson, and one that will stay with me for as long as I live. I just hope that I can heal enough to accept another person into my life in the future. But I can tell you one thing: I will be looking intently for the carefully concealed evidence that I ignored when I fell into the trap laid by a very crafty and skillful predator, and if I see any of the signs I will run as fast as I can in the other direction.

—Barbara Pederson

TWENTY YEARS TOO LONG

I MET MY EX-HUSBAND THE year before both of my parents died. My father had passed away and three months later I had a miscarriage. Three months later, my mother died. It was a difficult time for me and he was there.

I didn't know then that I was the perfect prey for a narcissist. I was vulnerable and had family money. Our first ten years together were uneventful, except that I had started taking on more of the financial responsibilities for the family because he was starting his own business and I wanted to help out. My care taking became a dominant aspect of our lives together. I thought I was in love. I was just setting myself up to be completely codependent and later abused.

Ten years into our marriage we moved. My daughter and I went ahead to find a home while my husband stayed behind to sell our condominium. She started school and I found a job. We settled into a nice routine. We'd been there for about a month when my husband joined us. The minute he walked into the house, I knew something was wrong. There was an energy that he brought into the house that just felt wrong. I couldn't put my finger on it, so I let it slide.

A few months later, after trying to talk to him, I asked him to leave. I suggested counseling, thinking we just needed to work on our marriage, but he refused. Actually he didn't really refuse, he just never responded, a ploy, I later learned, that he used to dominate through passive resistance. We remained married to keep up a façade for our daughter. I had a feeling that a divorce with him would be difficult, so I put it off for many years. Knowing he would fight me for full custody, I waited ten more years before filing. My daughter turned eighteen two months before we signed our divorce papers.

I had noticed that mutual friends had become distant a few years before my divorce. It was very subtle. I thought possibly I had done something or said something to offend them. I've learned we have a tendency to look at ourselves first to try to see what we did to "deserve" being ostracized or shunned. It rarely occurs that perhaps there is something else going on. Little did I know that they were being groomed as "flying monkeys."

Julie was the mother of my daughter's riding coach. We weren't good friends, but we had a friendly relationship. She and her daughter had taken my daughter to a foreign country for an international horseback jumping competition. Before they left, I asked them twice to let me know the phone number where I could reach them in case of an emergency. They never responded.

When they returned, I was angry that they had taken my daughter for seven days without telling me the name and number of the hotel where they were staying and let them know. Julie wrote to me, saying that if I hadn't written them an email telling them I never wanted to speak with them again, they would have responded. I didn't know what she was talking about. I had never written that email. I became very agitated and confused. This was the beginning of the gaslighting.

I wrote back and asked her for a copy of this email. She said she couldn't find it. I know she couldn't because it didn't exist. Then she wrote, "Your daughter is a wonderful person, it's too bad she has a mother like you." I was stricken. Reading that, I felt as if I had been hit in the stomach. I had no idea where all this animosity was coming from. Hurt and confused, I wrote to her daughter, asking what was going on. She replied, "We've heard about all the other times you've put your daughter through something like this." Something like what? Heard from whom? Now I knew something was terribly wrong.

Someone had said something about me behind my back to them, but I had no idea who and no idea what. It never occurred to me that it was my husband of fifteen years. It was so subtle and so passive-aggressive. I didn't put it together until reading a marital history during our divorce that demonized me and blamed me for everything. It was then that I put all the pieces together. He was the one behind the smear campaign.

I later learned that he told his attorney that I had been diagnosed with borderline personality disorder and that he was a nuclear physicist. I've learned since that he doesn't even have a bachelor of science. For years I thought he was an engineer by profession.

I still didn't have a label for what he'd done to me. I started researching online and learned about the various behaviors of narcissists. When I realized that he demonstrated many of the signs of narcissistic abuse, I knew that my abuse had a name. That is when my recovery started.

There is no doubt in my mind that my ex-husband has narcissistic tendencies, even though he has never been officially diagnosed. All the little things that didn't make sense, all the gut feelings that I had, all the red flags that I ignored finally made sense. It was narcissistic abuse.

I struggled accepting the reality of it. I couldn't believe that I had put up with the abuse for so long. I realized that every time he turned away when I entered a room, every time he talked to me with a demeaning tone of voice, every time he interrupted me, every time he said arrogantly "Like I told you ... ," it was abuse, plain and simple. I had to come to terms with that.

Compounding the abuse were smear campaigns, blaming, projection, and accusations that I abused our daughter. I started questioning my reality. I didn't know what was real and what was fabricated. I felt like a tangled ball of yarn, knotted up and confused.

I started to recall my childhood. The only thing my alcoholic mother was active with besides drinking was neglecting and ignoring me. My feelings were never validated and I took care of everyone. It was my way of dealing with a situation that was out of control.

I continued this behavior in my marriage and ended up "taking care" of my husband and my daughter, which is how I ended up feeling so unappreciated and invalidated. I wanted the love, acceptance, validation and appreciation that I never received from my parents. I got none of that with my husband, either. What I did get was a detailed marital history that accused me of molesting and abusing our daughter and blamed me completely for the breakdown of our marriage. My husband had written, "I became the object of her anger," portraying himself as the victim.

To top it off, I had to give him money because he couldn't earn a living, since he was 67 when we divorced. The man had worked his entire life, but had no savings and was living off of social security, $60,000 in debt. I had to pay off his debts, give him money, my house and my business. He was not satisfied until he had destroyed me.

I plead to anyone who even thinks they are involved with a narcissist: Leave. Leave as soon as you are able. Don't think you can rationalize your way out. Just leave. And don't look back.

It took me a good year and a half after my divorce to get my head on straight. I could not think coherently. I had no idea what I was feeling. I was in a daze. As time passed, I started feeling somewhat normal again, like my old self. I had no friends, no family, no home and no job. My daughter had started college and I was on my own for the first time in twenty years.

I will never be the same person as I was before meeting my ex-husband. I will be wiser, stronger, more compassionate and better off than I've ever been. I'm beginning to see the light at the end of the tunnel, despite the many times when I didn't think I would ever see that light.

It does get better—you just have to keep going and keep trusting. Don't let what happened to you make you into a bitter, disgruntled person. You are better than that. Take care of yourself. Love yourself.

I learned that it's time for me to take care of ME. It's time for me to love ME.

I have remained with no contact with my ex-husband since the divorce and I plan on keeping it that way. I have no doubt that his girlfriend is his new target. I would not be surprised if she called me one day and said, "Hey, can we talk?" My daughter maintains a relationship with him, so I minimize contact with her, lest he use her again to try to hurt me. I still live in fear of him, but he got what he wanted, so I think I've been discarded. I don't mind. As long as he's not in my life anymore.

Twenty years was too long.

—*Angela Dufresne*

MY ABUSIVE RELATIONSHIP: WHY I STAYED AND HOW I LEFT

ONE IN FOUR WOMEN WILL experience domestic violence in their lives. Two out of three female homicides are linked to domestic violence. Domestic violence has no boundaries; it isn't a cultural or ethnic problem. A victim can be young or old, rich or poor, highly educated or undereducated. I am a professional, successful female who only a few short months ago walked away from a 22-year marriage, my home and my life. Here is my story.

A state-mandated initiative was founded in 2000, requiring all municipal police departments to establish a Domestic Violence Crisis Team. In 2002, my local police department established a domestic violence team, consisting of police personnel and civilian volunteers, and I applied for and was accepted on this team.

I volunteered on the Domestic Violence Crisis Team for five years. Prior to applying for the team, I hadn't been in the workforce for several years. My spouse had convinced me to stay home to raise our two children. He didn't want me to volunteer for this team. Finally, after multiple arguments, he finally allowed me to join.

While going through our training for the domestic violence team, I saw many parallels in my life, especially when we discussed the "Power and Control" wheel in an abusive relationship. I kept quiet about these parallels. I was never physically harmed and I felt no one would understand.

He had put his hands around my neck and had held me down, but there were no bruises or broken bones. I had a very broken spirit. I convinced myself that the abuse going on in my marriage was normal. After my husband was verbally, emotionally, or sexually abusive to me, we would go through a "honeymoon period." I would get lavish gifts or be taken out to dinner to make up for the abuse. He would be extremely charming during this period. He knew exactly what to do and say to keep me under his control.

He would make me feel guilty and made me believe the abuse was my fault. The honeymoon period was often very short lived. I spent my life "walking on eggshells." I never knew when he was going to get angry.

My husband was extremely jealous, and there were daily accusations of affairs. I never cheated on him. I feared speaking to men. Over the years, I was stalked. My spouse monitored my emails, text messages, phone calls, voice mail, and my social media. I had no privacy. If I objected to his monitoring, I was accused of hiding something from him.

To destroy my confidence, my spouse compared me to younger, thinner models and actresses. He would discuss how "hot" television personalities were in front of my children, their friends, and me. He spoke about the women who had tried to "pick him up" during his day.

He convinced me to leave my job to stay home to raise our children. I'd had a good job. However, he felt we would do better financially if he started his own business. I ended up "working" for his new venture and never received a paycheck for any work I did. I had to be available whenever he called and "needed" me to work. I resented never receiving a paycheck. He demanded a lot for an unpaid employee. I was expected to stop whatever I was doing to work for him. I cancelled many of my children's play dates because he needed me to work. If I didn't change my plans to accommodate him, that would equate to hours of him complaining and berating me.

I had no access to money without asking him for it. I no longer had a bank account in my name. I had to provide receipts for everything I purchased. He would question essential household items. There were accusations of frivolous spending. To ensure my isolation, he would lend out my vehicle to his friends and family. He made sure on many occasions to leave me home without any money and without a vehicle. I was trapped and spiraled into depression. He would threaten to leave me when he was angry. I was afraid I would be penniless and homeless. He used that control tactic when our children were small. He wanted me to fear that he would leave me.

I was a very confident person when I met him. He destroyed me slowly and methodically. Over the years, I endured "gaslighting." Gaslighting is a technique an abuser uses to make their victim believe they are crazy. He lied constantly and when I confronted him about the lies, he would contort the truth until I believed him.

My spouse made sure I was isolated. The isolation started slowly, first isolating me from my family and then friends. He disliked anyone who encouraged me. Over the years, I met many acquaintances. However, these relationships never formed into friendships. My spouse always undermined potential relationships. Over the decades of our marriage, the abuse I endured was emotional, sexual, and contained years of control and isolation. I think the sexual abuse was the worst. I don't know if I will ever be whole again from that form of abuse.

A few years ago, my spouse's business had failed. It was his fifth business venture that had failed. Our family was financially struggling, so I went back to work. I started working part time and added more hours. In a few short years, I was working full time. My job quickly was becoming a professional career.

I started to rediscover my self-worth. However, I still had unresolved issues from living with someone who was never satisfied with me. I thought I was crazy, as my husband had told me time and again. I decided to see a therapist. I feared I would lose my career if my employer found out my secret that I was "crazy."

My husband belittled my career and my salary and felt I spent too much time at work. His efforts to undermine my career made me realize I was a victim of abuse. I was just beginning to build myself up and my job gave me passion in my life for the first time. I started therapy and realized I wasn't crazy. This was such a relief.

I suffered from anxiety, depression, PTSD and low self-esteem, stemming from years of abuse. I was very ill a few months ago with cardiac failure and was hospitalized. I went through months of medical testing and specialists. It was concluded that my illness was caused by living many years under extreme emotional stress. The years of abuse I endured had taken a toll on me spiritually, emotionally, and physically. I had a smile on my face, but my heart felt like it was torn from my chest.

Thanks to my career and therapy, I was able to start to rebuild my self-esteem and developed friendships. I recently walked away from my home, left my husband, and filed for divorce. After the hospitalization he realized he couldn't control me like he did before. He tried a few more times just prior to me leaving the house to demean and destroy me.

He "upped" his game during this time. He wanted to completely destroy my integrity. He tried to "Facetime" his male friend while we were engaged in a sexual act. He downloaded a picture from a porn site and stated he was very upset seeing ME in that way. He told my children the porn picture he downloaded was ME. It was obvious it wasn't ME. He insisted it was me because the woman in the video had a pair of shoes on similar to a pair that I once owned.

He tried to take pictures of me naked and demanded I pose for him. He kept pressuring me for nude pictures, and I kept refusing. He told me he wanted the pictures to show his friends. He asked me to perform sexual acts on his male friend while he watched. He pressured me about this daily. I wouldn't cave in to his craziness. I didn't acquiesce to any of these depraved demands. They were desperate measures from a desperate narcissist trying to destroy me anyway he could.

I am so glad I fled this relationship. I have my own place now, a safe haven. I am able to financially live on my own. It has been a struggle emotionally. After all the abuse I endured, I have days of ups and downs.

Domestic violence is not only physical abuse. Domestic violence is emotional abuse, sexual abuse, financial dependence, control, psychological abuse and gaslighting. Some of the signs of an abusive relationship are:

- Financial control: taking your money and not allowing you access to it. Counting every penny spent in the household.
- Isolation: jealousy of time spent with friends or family. Jealousy of time spent away from him/her.
- Destroying self-esteem: embarrassing or putting you down.
- Destroying your property or harming your pets.
- Telling you "You are a bad parent"; criticism of your parenting skills.
- Intimidating you with weapons and/or physical force.
- Preventing you from working or going to school.
- Sexual abuse: pressuring you to have sex or perform a sexual act you are uncomfortable with.
- Pressuring you to do drugs or alcohol.

I think back over those years and I am very grateful to have my wonderful children. My husband criticized me endlessly about my poor parenting skills. I know now that I am a good parent and my children know I love them. My children are the reason that I am taking back my life. I want them to see me as a strong survivor and not a victim.

Why did I stay? My self-esteem was ruined for a very long time. I was socially isolated from my family and friends. I kept everything that was going on in my marriage a secret. I feared for my safety if I left him. I was financially dependent on my spouse. I am an educated woman who was working towards a master's degree when I met him. He persuaded me to stop school after the birth of our first son. Eventually, he trapped me in his web of lies. I believe I suffered from Stockholm syndrome for many years.

It isn't easy to leave. Unless you have lived in an abusive relationship, a typical person wouldn't understand. It seems perfectly logical to an outsider that it would be easy to leave an abusive relationship. It truly isn't and walking away is terrifying for a victim.

No one deserves to live his or her life as a prisoner.

Love shouldn't hurt and abuse is not love.

—Mary Laumbach-Perez

CHAPTER 4

THE STRUGGLE FOR FREEDOM

Sometimes you have to let go to be free.

—Anonymous

THE TWO OPPOSITE SIDES OF KNOWING ABOUT NARCISSISM

IN MY CONTINUING EVALUATION OF where my life was, is, and appears to be going, I have discovered there are certain things that I know now that I sometimes wish that I didn't. While I wish that I didn't know them, I also understand that ultimately they are going to benefit me.

Confused enough yet? To be more to the point, I often wish that I didn't know anything about narcissistic personality disorder (NPD). Why? Let me explain.

My narcissistic wife (and now ex) moved out of our home nine months ago. This was in addition to us dating back in 1999, when she abruptly left me, dating again in 2001, when she again abruptly left me, and then getting together again in 2006 and ultimately getting married in 2009.

She also moved out without warning in November 2013, only to return in late January 2014, with the final move out occurring in August of 2014. She got married in between both of our dating periods in '99 and '01, meaning that, including me, she has been married four times (before she was 36). I knew nothing about NPD until December 2014. I only discovered it while researching information on my own dysfunction of codependence.

With the history out of the way, let me get to the point. When I knew nothing about narcissism, I always had hope that she would return to me. After all, she had done it so many times before and I always felt there had to be a way to make things better so she wouldn't leave again. I didn't like her leaving, but I always seemed to find that way to "make things better," at least enough for her to come back.

When you are as in love with someone as much as I was with her, you are both willing and able to do about anything to please that person. The same thought process was in place following her most recent departure in August of last year. I was convinced it was just a matter of time before she determined how much she missed and needed me, and that she would want to come back.

We had so much incredible history and so many amazing memories (this really is true, at least from my perspective) that she just couldn't avoid knowing we were meant to be together. After all, she had told me that exact thing so many times, including that she wanted to grow old together with me, and that I "was hers." The absolute hope in her return was always there. That hope was always there until …

I mentioned that I learned about NPD by accident when researching my own codependent dysfunction (which was identified during counseling that I initiated as a result of my wife moving out—the problem had to be with me, right?).

The more I researched NPD, the more the irrational suddenly became rational, the more I could connect the dots of what she had done over the years, and the more I knew she couldn't be fixed and would never stop doing what she was doing.

The hope that I held that she would return again was suddenly GONE. I still don't want to believe that she has NPD, but so many of the symptoms apply, and her history agrees with nearly everything about the disorder.

I was once convinced that when she did something that she and I had shared, she would always have to think about me in some manner. That seemed to give me some level of solace, but now that is gone too.

A perfect example of this thought process occurred just today. There is a local donut shop that I introduced her to which we frequented often, one of the many "rituals" that we had. Don't underestimate the rituals either, as we were constantly on the go and had so many things that defined "us" (or at least that is what I was led to believe).

Anyway, today as I was passing the donut shop, I noticed her car in the lot (and no, I didn't stop—I avoid her at this point). Prior to knowing about NPD, I would have gotten some level of satisfaction thinking that there had to be a thought or memory of me when she was there. Now, I no longer think that and feel that nothing that we did meant anything to her, and that she wouldn't hesitate to do those very same things with someone else exactly the way that she and I used to do them. Yes, she does have a new companion, and that she is likely doing these things with him is not lost on me.

The bottom line is that before I knew about NPD, I always had some level of hope that she would want to return to me simply because she did love me, that she did value what we had accomplished, the memories were sweet, and that I was truly special and what she wanted.

Since knowing about NPD, that hope is completely gone, replaced with the knowledge that even if she does contact me and desires to come back (which she likely will at some point) it is not for reasons that a "normal" person would feel (i.e., for love, caring, sentimentality, and a real need to reconnect with someone who she shouldn't have disconnected from in the first place). It is simply out of convenience and the need for the best "supply" that she can find at a given time. That, my friends, is just sad and depressing for both of us, but especially for me, in that I am the only one that understands it that way.

Is it better to not know about NPD and simply continue to have hope, or is it better to know and run away as fast as one can? For me, I am caught between the two, continuing to have hope in some kind of miracle that her NPD either disappears or she is able to understand and work with it, while knowing that I should run away as fast as I can, but am unable to do so.

It's a tough place to be and quite frankly, I am tired of being here. I am working on it, but it is a much slower process than one could hope for.

—*A. P. Heart*

LOSING A NARCISSIST: THE LONELIEST FEELING EVER

THE CHALLENGES OF A RELATIONSHIP breakup are never easy. Breaking up with (or rather losing) a narcissist is so much worse that it cannot be compared with a "normal" breakup. I have all the evidence that I need, as I am in the middle of such an event. I say the middle because lately, every day has felt just like the day before, and the next day usually feels the same too.

My breakup is in month seven and started when my wife of five years moved out in August. This was not unexpected, as she had also moved out with no warning in November of 2013 (only to move back in February of 2014). I was not aware that narcissism was a true personality disorder until December of 2014, so it is fairly new to me, but it also has made a lot of senseless things at least understandable (although still senseless and irrational). Sadly, knowing about the disorder DOES NOT take away the pain and anxiety of the breakup and post breakup process.

Our divorce appears to be nearing the end in that we—and by "we" I mean our attorneys—are negotiating the final assets and liabilities. Just typing those words is a difficult and confusing thing to do, hence my loneliness about losing my narcissistic wife. My emotional (and irrational) side still, after all of the deceitful, mean, underhanded things that she has done in the last seven months, doesn't want to lose her.

I still wake up in an empty house that we bought together wondering what happened. Over the last several years, we have made so many incredible memories and they are all that I can seem to think about. They are constantly on my mind, replaying like a DVD player stuck in the repeat mode. Everywhere I look or every place I go, I can seem to make some kind of connection to her and off my mind goes down that undesirable path of questions, wondering how I got here, and struggling greatly with what is going to follow. Yes, I can bring myself back to reality and think about the menacing, devaluing, and the incredibly mean discarding that she has done, but it only lasts so long before those pleasant (and apparently invalid) memories return.

Working in the same location as her certainly doesn't help my feelings of vulnerability. I can always tell when some new "bad" thing is about to happen, as her behavior noticeably changes.

I have done my best to implement no contact with her over the last two and a half months, although this is extremely hard to do when you work in the same building. Since I have done that, her demeanor has changed considerably, as she appears to be trying very hard to avoid me more than I avoid her. She didn't do this prior to implementing no contact and in fact she would go out of her way to make herself visible to me as much as possible, to "show" me what I didn't have anymore, to inflict as much pain and agony as possible.

With that said, over the last couple of days, her avoidance of me has increased even more than usual, with her not even looking up anytime she senses my presence, even if just walking by. As expected, the bad news to follow was more asinine demands from her and her attorney, with her yet again exposing her grandiose sense of entitlement and asking for things she has no business asking for.

I am not sure why I even get surprised anymore, since in the last seven months she has shown no remorse, guilt, empathy, conscience, caring, or any other feeling that a "normal" person would. I know: why would I even care about someone like that?

With that comes my loneliness. I was married to a woman who appeared too perfect to be true and, in fact, was. Her three previous marriages (before she was 30) should have been ample warning. Every day, I try to look forward, telling myself it is going to get better, praying to God that He help me with this, that He deliver me from this unrelenting confusion.

Some days are better than others, but there continues to be an abnormal sense of loss, a sense that I did everything wrong and that she is somehow totally innocent. That is the unseen danger of the narcissist. They leave you questioning your worth, your sanity, and your ability to consider any kind of future without them. I am committed to get through this, as I really have no other options.

Like a fool, I selflessly ventured out onto thin ice to be with this woman, clearly hearing the cracking and splintering surface, yet going further and further out into the deep water, only to fall through when I thought I was in a safe place, left hopelessly floundering, helplessly gasping for air.

When I look up, I see her standing there looking down at me, staring, contemplating, yet making no effort to help in any way. Her face is emotionless, barren, with no recognition of who I am or what we have done, wondering if there is anything else she could or should take from me before walking away, leaving me to sink below the surface. Truly, that is my loneliness and somehow I still love her, but I don't want her.

—*A. P. Heart*

THE POWER OF CHOICE

"Please help me," I say from the core of my soul,
Which is battered and bruised from the hideous control.
Domestic Violence is terrorism in the heart and home
It is the most suppressed kind of torture I've ever known.

Abuse doesn't always arrive in a loud, roaring tone.
Sanctimoniously whispered, its intent not shown.
It's horrific. It's cruel. It's crippling and mean.
It's destruction, dysfunction, mind-control not seen.

The silence is piercing, terrorism is imminent.
Like waiting on the plate for the ball to be pitched.
No idea of direction, speed, or strength.
On guard I wait, to cover my base.

The curve ball from left is what I expect.
The attack so severe, the defense so weak.
Moments of fear, destruction and torture.
"Your tears are a weapon" ... as I cry and don't speak.

Strike one. I'm down and nowhere to run.
Face the onslaught of what's about to take place.
Reading the play, as it churns in my soul,
"You have no credibility" ... I miss again to save face.

Strike two. I beg, yet not on my knees,
Time ticking by with anticipation high.
Power and control are reigning supreme.
"You will not scream" ... but I will not lie.

Strike three. I'm out. Its time to go.
The punishing silence, the push, the pain.
Game over, I choose life over death.
"It's MY life" I say, my safety will remain.

It starts up again as I leave the ballpark.
The memories, the injustice, the right to survive.
In the lounge room, the bedroom, the courtroom, I pray.
With children and scars, I thank God we're alive.

With dread, fright and panic that his lawyers instill.
These bullying tactics are no longer to be.
Change is essential and focus I must,
As others have sacrificed the ultimate before me.

Entrapment beckons with lawyers in tow.
But no one to stand up and say, "This is wrong."
Only me to decide what is to be,
The road being tedious, tumultuous and long.

Growing tired and exhausted, weary and sore.
With no money left to pay the huge legal bill.
Nothing to hide and proud to be me,
All I have is my children, my dignity and will.

With chains and roadblocks, it doesn't matter any more.
I've been through the tunnels of torment before.
With my children alongside in the darkness of horror.
Change on the cusp of what is in store.

A writer I am, no fear in my words.
Erin Brockovich, Bono or Geldof I'm not.
Just a brave little person breaking the silence,
On a life of fear, intimidation and violence.

With courage I stride, gathering kindness from many.
Speak up I will for me to grow tall.
My heart in tatters, my spirit crushed.
Trying to stop the pain of it all.

For my children and me
We wear no shame.
We are wholesome and good
Not scapegoats for blame.

The silence is broken; the wisdom is known
The barriers removed, the door no longer shut.
There's no turning back in the darkest of tunnels
It's too dark to reveal the deepest of cuts.

In a world of self-battles, delusion and grandeur.
The terrorist lives on but not on TV.
It takes strength, courage and the will to survive,
Plus the power of choice to say
"NO"... . he's not living with me.

Strike me once, I chose to cry in pain.
Strike me twice, I chose to run and save face.
Strike me three times, I chose to walk the path of safety with my children,
my pride and my battered soul to fight for our freedom.

Strike me never again.

—*E. J. Mason*

A COVERT NARCISSIST

I WAS JUST LOOKING FOR a fellow-Christian friend who I could hang out with and discuss biblical dialogue with. My ad read, "Christian Woman, 47 years of age, looking for a Christian friend who is kind, friendly, and enjoys discussing the bible." He sent me an email with a picture. He was 60 years of age.

We emailed back and forth quite a bit, then talked on the phone. I was very open about my Christian beliefs and what kind of person I was. His reply was always, "Me too! Me too! I've been looking for a Christian friend who actually 'walks the talk.'"

He continued to call every night, and sometimes in the morning as well. He pressed to meet me soon, so we met at a diner. He brought with him a little pad and a pen to ask me questions. I just thought, "That's different," but I liked him. He seemed so much like me.

Every question that I answered, he replied, "Me too!" Afterwards, he gave me the biggest, tightest hug I'd had in a very long time. It felt really good! He began texting me, along with constant calls. He wanted to get together again. We were developing feelings for each other beyond friendship after one meeting, thanks to his constant calls, emails, and texts.

He mentioned how beautiful I was inside and out. He had looked for a woman just like me for a long time. We met a second time, and a red flag came up. After our very first romantic kiss, he said joyfully, "I'm looking for true love, and until you came along, I had never found it. Even with my last wife, I only married her out of lust, but it wasn't true love."

I should have run away then and not looked back. (He also claimed that his first wife "beat him up all the time.") He swooned me daily in texts, calls, and emails. I buried the Red Flag and continued into a relationship with him. We were so much alike!

He started telling me things that made my heart beat faster: "You are my soul mate," "Before you, I'd never truly loved anyone," "I love you more than life itself," and "Let's get married in a year, exactly on Valentine's Day!"

Though I was on cloud nine, something in my gut was nudging me, now and then—a suspicion. So, one evening while he was sleeping, I looked into his past emails with others. There were sexual messages back and forth to people on Craigslist.

One in particular was about him making plans to have sex with another man's wife, while the man watched. They were making concrete plans! Shocked, I brought it to his attention. He excused it all away by saying that was before he met me, and it was a time that he had "fallen away from God." Again, I should've run away from him, as fast as I could.

Instead, I accepted his excuse and also his anger at the fact that I went through his cell phone. In fact, there was no more talk about his emails and the devious behavior they contained, but instead, it was all about how bad of a person I was to look at his email.

As time went on, I found his laptop history with pictures of naked college girls. Lots of them. I brought it to his attention, and the next time I looked on his laptop history, there was a site he had gone onto that said, "How to surf the Internet privately without leaving a trail."

He started accusing me of viewing porn and cheating on him, and whenever he failed to validate me, and I called him on it, he said I was delusional or psychotic. I found that he had been sexting other women and going on dating sites as well, while still claiming his unquenchable love for me.

When we'd get into arguments, he'd call me "bitch," "slut," "loser," "a joke," "a thief," or say that I was "using him." He told me that he once had an addiction to big breasts, but learned how to curb his lusts. He said so many hurtful things to me, and when I told him how much it hurt, he said it was my problem for having such low self-esteem.

I had to call the police on him one evening when he held me down, a mean and crazy look in his eyes. The harder I tried to get away, the tighter his grip became, and the more he dug his nails into my wrists. The next day, I had bruises and scratches all over my arms. His excuse: "I just wanted you to appreciate me more."

Everything was always my fault, no matter what he did or said. He was never accountable. He even told me that I was possessed by three demons and that they wanted him gone because he had so much "light" in him.

He said his "spiritual gift" was discernment, and he always seemed to "bring out the demons in other people." I figured that meant that he made a lot of people very angry. After I left him, he began his hoovering. His love-bombing was intense. He "needed me," and "would never search for another if I left him," and in fact, "would wait for me to come to my senses, no matter how long that took."

I told him we'd give it another try, and his reply was that he was in love with a 29-year-old Russian woman, who had a poignant story, and that he wanted to marry her. I was confused, angry, and crushed. It turned out that this "29 year old Russian beauty" was a scam. Yet, he told me that he still kept her "steamy pictures" that she sent him, and wanted to know if I wanted to come over and look at them with him.

I finally broke it off after that final straw. He hoovered some more, then did a final discard on me. In less than a week, he had a new girlfriend. I'm still trying to move on from all the depravity, deception, and abuse of this covert narcissist.

—Tamara Yancosky-Moore

THE WAR THAT WAGES WITHIN

How do I fight it—
The war that wages within?
When I dare hope that
I have defeated it;
maybe now it will leave me;
maybe now I can walk back,
retracing my footsteps to a place
and time when I didn't feel
this heavy weight around my neck,
when I could talk without
tears finishing my sentences,
when I could smile and laugh—
when I was NORMAL.
When I gather bits of my confidence
and take faltering steps
on this path to normalcy
it springs upon me
from the shadows where it lurks,
hidden inside the recesses of my mind.
It mocks my attempts;
it turns all my rationality on its head
and I again feel stranded
on this island of desolation,
unending and unreasonable tears
threatening to drown my resolve to live.
I paralyze with the suddenness
and enormity of this grief,
Unable to see the path,
my eyes blurred with tears.

No longer having a place to go,
I take refuge on my side of bed.
I cuddle in blanket of inertia,
hugging a pillow of helplessness.
My strength saps,
my resolve breaks.
I do not hear my heart beat,
I do not feel my soul.
It's just darkness.
I no longer feel human.
Merely my shadow
and nothing more.
I look in the mirror and see
my eyes staring back,
like the eyes of a person dead.
Do others also see it?
I wonder how they recognize me
and still call me by my name.
For days I live in the same room,
in the same bed,
in the same corner.
I dare not go out.
I live like a social recluse;
a leper.
My lesions do not show on my skin,
for I hide them from others,
lest they see them and shun me,
or worse, cover them
with the wrong bandages
that hurt more than they heal.
What is this trial where
I accuse and convict myself?
I suffer the punishments, too,
but still the trial doesn't end.

It starts all over again,

convicting and punishing

over and over.

This cesspool of grief, remorse, regret:

will I ever get out of it?

—Dr. Shalini Singh

ALPHA AND OMEGA

LOOKING BACK, I SHOULD HAVE seen the signs. Red flags were everywhere. Instead I adored a man who had occasional outbursts. Who called me a "stupid bitch" for not aborting our firstborn. Who would spit in my face because his dinner was cold. Who almost talked me into killing myself. Who cheated on me with multiple women. Who committed fraud. Who bought and sold drugs. Who had a restraining order against him from a previous ex. Who stole over $10,000 from an employer before he was even eighteen.

By the time I figured all this out, it was too late. I was broken.

I met my ex-husband in 1998. Eleven months after "knowing" him, we married and I was pregnant. During those eleven months, he told me that his parents were dead. The only family that I met was the family who I now refer to as the "normal side": wonderful, educated, morally grounded.

After we married, in a most peculiar meeting, I met his mother. She lived in a trailer in the middle of nowhere, surrounded by cats. When I say "cats," I don't mean a few cats; I mean there were cats on top of the trailer, inside the trailer, in the air-conditioning vents—everywhere. I felt like I had walked into a Stephen King book.

After our daughter was born, his mother and long-lost sister moved in with us. It was a small two-bedroom apartment, and with them sleeping on my living room floor, all their possessions in garbage bags, I quickly had enough.

He responded by convincing me that it was best for our children if I quit my stable job and moved with him to a family-owned home in the middle of nowhere. I was told that it was the only way to get his mom and sister to leave. That was a lie.

For one year, the kids and I lived in the middle of nowhere, with little to no contact with family or friends. I was placed on a strict budget of $100.00 a week for the kids and I to survive on. He was never home, always "working."

When he was home, it was hell. I walked on eggshells, terrified of upsetting him. I call that year the "breaking-down" phase. One weekend, he came home and saw that I was looking at jobs and apartments and questioned why I would dare to defy him and be so ungrateful. He always told me that I was ungrateful.

To keep me submissive, he bought me a house in the best city in our state, which had the top schools. I was finally back in civilized, suburban America. And I was pregnant again. To keep my attention diverted from him, I was "allowed" to go to the gym daily. I balanced the checking account (that I knew about). I went to lunch with my friends and socialized with other business owner's wives.

We had the picture-perfect family and life, as long as I didn't question his morals, speak of what happened behind closed doors, and never contradicted his reality. I spent every day trying to make him happy, no matter the cost or sacrifice. When I would make a mistake that upset him, I spent anywhere from a week to a month in what I refer to as the "glass box." It's an invisible box that I was put in and denied any human contact, until I admitted my wrongdoings.

When my youngest child was two, my husband had a "mental break." He removed us from his health insurance and demanded that I get a job, or he was going to make sure we lost the house. I did as I was told and got a good job. He felt that his hold was slipping and I, like him, wanted a divorce.

He didn't expect that reaction. He changed. His change led to the best eight months of our marriage. I was showered in gifts, diamonds, vehicles (two), flowers, body massages, and great, considerate sex. There was one unexpected twist. He had a mistress that wasn't happy with him "saving" his marriage and ending their affair.

She wasn't like the other women that I'd previously dealt with, and there were many women. He couldn't deny her claims. She was cruel. She enjoyed calling me at my job, telling me she had been in my home. My kids meant nothing to her. She hated me. However, she opened my eyes a bit. I began to disobey: I snooped, questioned fiercely, and began to see him for the monster he truly is.

It took me five more years to learn whom I was married to. He had convinced me to go to marriage counseling for our children. He swore that she was gone and he would never cheat, lie, or betray me again. Another lie.

After I discovered he resumed his affair with her, I went to see our therapist. He sat me down and told me I was married to a sociopath. I had no idea what that meant. I was trained to believe everything was my fault. I was a horrible person, who didn't deserve the slightest act of kindness in any form. I deserved everything he did. I deserved the panic and anxiety attacks. I was stupid, worthless, fat, ugly, and should die. I stayed in therapy during the end of the marriage, plotting my escape with the therapist. I had myself tested for STDs and was put on medication to help with the thoughts of suicide and panic attacks. I became outspoken and didn't cringe at being put into the "glass box." Finally, I packed all of his things, threw him out, and filed for a divorce.

I was free!

He would become her problem and they could focus their attention on each other. I was wrong. Four years divorced, and I am still seen as property. Not just by him though, by her as well.

A woman that I will have nothing to do with is completely obsessed with me. She tries to look like me, dress like me, and demands we be friends for the children. She stalks me online, emails me pretending to be him, signs her name to legal documents as my children's mother, continuously lies about me, and demands that I do as she says.

When I told him that I hated him, he tried to burn my shed down. They have taken my kids out of the state in the middle of the night because I purchased a new car. I have had my home and car broken into. I have been told descriptive details about the slaughter of my dogs. I have filed nine police reports, but it hasn't stopped.

I am constantly told to continue reporting; don't stop reporting. The advice I get is to stay off-line, never leave my home alone, keep my doors locked, delete all my email accounts, sell my house and leave the state with my children.

I don't run. I never have and I never will.

My children have two therapists: one to help them cope, the other to teach them how to protect themselves. I also have two therapists: one therapist to help me deal with him and the other I tell things to that had happened during the marriage that I will not tell anyone else. My children fear him killing me, and my youngest stays on guard if we are all in the same place. My oldest hasn't spoken a word to him in four years. My daughter, now the target, has learned to hide her emotions.

I am meeting my attorney the day after tomorrow. I will be free. I will date again without fearing that my home will be burned down. I will not worry about what I say online, fearing threats and retaliations. I will not be obsessively careful with my actions and behavior out of the fear of looking crazy and losing my children to these people.

I will one day live my life like everyone else: without fear of this covert narcissist.

—Joan Rice

IN MY SHOES

Naked, cold, frightened, bare feet, hungry inside, empty, lost.

In my shoes; that is how I felt with you.

There was no love, I wanted you to hold me and to talk to me like an adult, not a child.

I was your wife, yet you didn't respect me.

You never cared, never said how sorry you were.

For just once, I would like for you to feel what was it like to be me: the pain, the loss.

It is not about you and me; we were supposed to be a family.

What happened to that dream?

You used it and recklessly abused it.

Finally you couldn't get enough. That's when I died inside.

Handcuffed, sitting in that courtroom, I wanted you to feel what was it like to be me.

You showed no emotion.

You still deny your crime; will you ever learn with time?

Naked, cold, frightened; how does it feel?

Bare feet, hungry inside, empty and lost.

I hope you get to feel; I hope you get to see

For even one day on this Earth how it does feel to be me.

—*Karen Reyna*

CHAPTER 5

ON PARENTAL NARCISSISM

Anyone can have a child and call themselves a parent. A real parent is a person who puts their child above their own selfish needs and wants.

—Anonymous

WHO DOES SHE BELONG TO?

MY MOTHER GAVE BIRTH TO four children. Her first child was stillborn. Her next two children were live births, and they were well loved. Mama's final birth was also a live birth. This baby was wanted and was needed, but not for the reasons most mothers have a baby. This child was planned, just as the previous three. Mama's life was hers, and everything was always completed on her schedule. Even pregnancies.

The pregnancy was wanted, because after the first three babies, Daddy decided that he'd had enough of Mama, so he left. No one was allowed to leave Mama! So, she followed him to Atlanta, Georgia, to talk him into coming home. That very weekend, she got pregnant. In essence, this baby was a tool. A game piece. Daddy wouldn't leave Mama if she were pregnant. Mama knew that. Her fourth baby was a trap that Mama needed to get Daddy to come home.

This fourth baby was me.

I wasn't pretty like Mama's other babies. They were beautiful, eight-pound cherubs with sparkly eyes and round cheeks. I weighed six pounds and wasn't healthy. In fact, I had such bad asthma that the doctor told Mama to have me baptized because I probably wouldn't live very long.

I have possibly three good memories of my childhood that are directly relative to my life. I have many beautiful memories that center around the events of my sister's life: her beauty pageants, her boyfriends, her proms, her dates, her wedding, her pregnancies. The memories even include her clothes and the music she listened to.

My brother had his own life. My memories of him are few, but for a while, he, too, was a Golden Child, like my sister. However, like me, he wasn't liked by Daddy, so he left home at a young age. Before he went, Mama showered him with love and gifts. Even after he'd left, I repeatedly heard how wonderful he was and how he could do no wrong.

I don't remember gifts being given to me as a child. I do remember hearing that my birthday was too close to Income Tax Day and that there was no money. At least that's what Mama always said. Mama said lots of things. She told many stories and always had a captive audience.

I'm not sure when I heard Mama's favorite story the first time, but I can tell you that she still tells it now, even as she is saddled with dementia. She still tells it with ease, and her description is painfully true. As she always had, Mama will tell the story to anyone who will listen, even if they've heard it before.

"We went to town today, and it happened again! I was walking through the grocery store and this lady stopped me! She wanted to tell me how beautiful my children are! She said Denise looked like a doll! Like painting a picture, she began by saying how her eyes were shaped. I can't even describe them! Dark eyes, with dark lashes, and the little nose was perfect! And look at her mouth!! It looks just like Cupid's bow! And it's topped off by the color of her skin and perfect hair! Why, I don't think I've ever seen a little girl so beautiful! You should enter her in a beauty contest! She is sure to win! And look at your handsome son! He looks like a perfect little gentleman! Those eyes and cheeks are adorable! He is just gorgeous! They could be on TV! And the way you have them dressed just makes them even more perfect! You must be so proud."

Everyone always listened to see what she would say next! All eyes were on Mama as she finished the story.

As she concludes her story, the tone in her voice changes. She will turn to me and pause as they wait to hear what the stranger said about me. Inevitably, Mama's audience also turns their eyes toward me, the child with long stringy hair, usually in braided pigtails, that I had done myself, with one braid longer than the other.

My bangs looked like they had been cut with hedge clippers. I was straight up and down skinny, and I was always told that my knees were the biggest part of my body. And I had a space between my front teeth that was large enough to drive a semi truck through.

There was nothing pretty about me, especially when I was being compared to the others.

No one would say a word. They only waited for Mama to finish her tale. You could sense how uncomfortable everyone was as they waited for Mama's next words:

"Who does SHE belong to?" Mama's question would be raised as she pointed to me.

I can still hear the laughter of Mama and the shame ringing in my ears. Mama's laughter cued her audience that they were to laugh as well. And they nearly always did.

I heard that story so many times that it's hard to figure out when I first began to notice a pattern.

In the story, I was actually on one side, and my siblings were on the other.

Mama would describe my brother and sister and point to one side of the room. When she got to me, the punch line, she actually pointed to the other side of the room.

Even in her story, I was separated from my family. That's how my entire life has felt.

I was never truly part of Mama's family, and she taught my brother and sister that this was acceptable. As children tend to do, they followed Mama's example, and anytime they deemed that I didn't fit in, for any reason, I was removed from the picture.

I may be a character in the stories of their lives, but I am absent in many chapters.

Despite the neglect that I suffered, actually likely because of the neglect that I suffered, I was always anxious to prove myself as a faithful and loving daughter. I'm certain that I believed that after an act of devotedness, Mama would somehow see how valuable I was and shower me with the love and affection that I yearned for.

Take for instance the time Mama needed her gallbladder removed. I was the one that drove her to the emergency room. I stayed with her while they diagnosed her and then performed surgery. I stayed the night with her, and the following day, and the following four days, because I knew better than to suggest that I needed to leave.

I had a child and a husband, but I knew that if I left, I would face the wrath of Mama. Finally, on the fourth day, I said that I needed to run to my house because I had to pay a bill. On the way back to the hospital, I got a flat tire. There were no cell phones then. By the time I walked to a place with a phone, had my husband come change the tire, paid the bill and went back to the hospital, I was in trouble.

"In trouble." I was 31 years old, and yet I was "in trouble." Mama told me when I got to the hospital that I obviously didn't want to help her, so I should leave. Despite explaining what had happened and the fact that I'd been by her side nonstop for four days, she called me a liar and told me to leave. I should have been happy that I could go home to my family, but I felt as though I'd been punched in the gut. That time, Mama didn't speak to me for about three weeks.

I also recall one of the many times that Mama and Daddy moved into my home that I shared with my family. Mama never could manage money, so she moved in with us during her low points. Of course, she always told everyone that she was moving in with us because we were having financial issues and needed her help. In reality, she didn't even contribute to the power bill.

During this particular stay, she began telling me that Daddy needed a new bed. She would tell me that every day. I asked her what she wanted to do about it, and she would always repeat, "Your father needs a new bed."

I finally got the strength to tell Mama that I had a larger bed in the barn. I told her that I knew she couldn't physically move it into the house, so I offered to bring it in. I also told her that she could go to the furniture store, buy a bed, and they would deliver it. Simple, right?

Mama got into her car and drove away.

No one heard from her for weeks.

Finally, I was told that she had rented an apartment with my niece and her boyfriend.

But what about Daddy, you wonder?

Mama left him at my house for over a year, and kept his paycheck. She gave him $100.00 a month to live on.

Daddy got very sick and decided to give my husband and myself power of attorney. When he told Mama, she had him moved into the laundry room of her apartment within 24 hours.

All of that over a bed ... or so it seemed.

That time, Mama didn't speak to me for almost fourteen years.

Now, Mama has dementia. For some reason, this has been a sort of release for me. The damage that she did to me is still here. I fight it daily. But now Mama is pitiful and even if she tries to manipulate, her mind isn't clear enough anymore to be good at it.

About two months ago, she was in the hospital and was very ill. I walked in and she immediately began to beg for forgiveness. She told me that she knew she had been a horrible mother to me. She told me that she was sorry.

I had never heard those words in my life. She also talked about how beautiful I am. I wondered if she'd had a stroke and it destroyed the "mean part" of her brain. Either way, I had prayed all of my life that Mama would be able to have peace in her mind.

I knew that despite her apparent disregard for me, it must have been torture to be her, as she was constantly planning your next move and next story. She seemed to have found that peace when I visited her that day.

As for me and my peace? I am so thankful that I possess compassion and forgiveness, for two reasons. Firstly, so that I know that I'm not like her. Secondly, so that I can forgive and move forward, despite bearing the scars of her emotional damage to me.

My relationship with my family is akin to being hit by a bus. The damage has been done. Hating the bus or the driver won't make me heal any faster. In fact, it just may slow me down.

Who do I belong to? I belong to myself.

—*Laura McCall*

THE INTERNAL DIALOGUE OF ONE CHILD
RAISED BY A PREDATORY CLUSTER B FAMILY

HAVE YOU EVER WONDERED WHAT it's like for a child raised by a predator? Ever been curious about what happens to those babies? I mean do they grow up to be predators themselves? After all, monkey see, monkey do, right? You are about to glimpse a tattered, faded snapshot of one little girl who just wanted to be loved and not exploited. Let us briefly peek at who and what she grew up to be.

We can all imagine ... Newborn babies crying with their whole hand wrapped around our pinky. Toddlers learning how to say their colors: wed, broo, lello, owenj, back, and gween. Kids, so trusting.

Impressionable children wondering and even dreaming of big, bright lives filled with laughter, play dates, and trips to the park. Learning how to draw stick figures with smiles, never quite getting the fingers to look like fingers. For those born of predators and personality disordered parents, social skills, life lessons and goal setting are an uphill battle of disciplines attempted well into adulthood.

Documented below is the inner dialogue of an adult child in her forties, raised by a Cluster B family. She is currently in her second decade of recovery from severe childhood trauma, including sexual abuse and exploitation at the hands of her loved ones.

"Maybe they don't know what they're doing ... Maybe they really do love me and just don't know how to show it. I mean, parents are supposed to love and nurture their babies. Mommies and daddies play with their kids and teach them how to grow up into healthy adults someday. If they really, really, really knew me or took a moment to see me for who I really am—deep down. If they could see my heart and how pure it is, and how it shatters with every lie, act of violence or unkind word. If they could hear my sincere words of compassion in response to their manipulative rants. If they would just stop and realize how deeply their selfish

words and actions wound me to the core of my being. If they only knew me ... maybe they would not have abused me. Maybe they would have really loved me, the way other kids' parents loved them. Maybe if they knew me, I would have lived a life filled with kindness, love, family outings, fun activities, planting flowers, laughing, playing, swimming, running through the sprinklers on a hot summer day, mud pies in the back yard, finger-painting on weekends ... My artwork might have been on the fridge ... They would have been at all my school plays or open house events. They would have seen me sing the national anthem on the 50 yard line of the stadium before the homecoming game, or the medal I won at that swim meet would have been acknowledged. Sitting first chair in concert orchestra for years and competing internationally would have warranted a congratulatory comment. If only. Maybe I wouldn't have had my innocence stolen from me more times than I care to think about. If they only knew how messed up I would be for decades. If they knew the years of ongoing abuse was permanently damaging my brain, maybe they would have stopped. If they knew I would go on to live with severe anxiety and debilitating posttraumatic stress. If they knew I would contemplate suicide a dozen times just to escape the pain of the memories. Maybe then ... they wouldn't have hurt me and scarred me forever ..."

That is a very disturbing internal dialogue. I know. Because that girl is me.

My name is Athena Moberg and I am a survivor advocate. I speak, educate, and write books for adult survivors of childhood sexual abuse. I've dedicated my life to not only studying and learning how to be healthy, but also finding ways to help other survivors do the same. I was failing at being a good mother, so I got help. I was failing at being a good wife, so I got help. I was failing at being a successful businesswoman, so? Yes, I got the help I needed to be all the woman God created me to be. Was it easy? Oh how I wish our recovery was easy. I fight. And when I am weary, I fight some more. And when I can no longer fight, I pray. I am learning more and more how to pray first. I am proud to be a lifelong student and spend my spare time finding ways to replace that disturbing internal dialogue with encouraging words of Truth.

One of the most painful truths I've learned over the years is that not everyone "cares" about others deeply. Not every human has the capacity for empathy and compassion. Not every person has the ability to experience tender feelings, act on them, see, care, dream, hope, and love. You see, what I've learned through speaking, educating, studying and eventually becoming certified through the National Alliance on Mental Illness is that NPD, Cluster B, narcissistic, psychopathic, and sociopathic individuals are literally not capable of empathy; it is in fact a chemical impossibility. That last sentence could be the most painful one of all, as I have dreamt my entire life of having a kind and loving family. All I can do now is hope, pray, and maintain healthy boundaries while pressing into my faith. I have been blessed with a global community of adult survivors of child abuse whom I serve daily through books, videos, and podcasts. Today, they are precisely what keep me alive. With the help of my wonderful husband, I am grateful to have broken the cycle of predatory behavior and abuse in my family.

—*Athena Moberg, CPC*

CELL MEMORY

ON A GRAY, FRIGID DAY in Cleveland, extreme pain had driven her to yet another new physician and another cold exam room. Having to remove her clothes made her feel as if she were somewhere else, leaving her body behind.

Her new doctor, a rheumatologist who appeared to be like her, mid-fifties, carefully pressed each of sixteen points on her body that would help to diagnose an agonizing condition called fibromyalgia. She hoped that was all it was. The medical student in the exam room looked on with interest. She hated going to the doctor. Actually, truth be told, she had the beginnings of a panic attack anytime someone unfamiliar touched her body, invading her private space.

As expected, the new MD began the history piece of the exam. She responded matter-of-factly, practically in a monotone. "Do you feel safe in your home? Has anyone ever verbally and emotionally abused you? Has anyone physically abused you?"

The doctor's response to her replies was unexpected as he stated, "Apparently you've had a great deal of therapy, as you are not crying or falling apart." Was that supposed to be good news? A compliment of some sort? His unexpected response was a first for her, that's for sure.

Here is what she learned that day: even with a list of therapists too long to remember, the cell memory of her mother's physical and emotional abuse had internalized her pain to the point that her immune system could not protect her from the years and years of agony and torment her mother had inflicted on her mind and body. Now she fully processed the term "cell memory."

These unwanted, unruly memories that had been extracted from an infant's mind via hypnosis, a child's mind via regression, a teenager's mind via psychoanalysis and an adult's mind via cognitive therapy would always represent just the tip of the iceberg when it came to healing her soul.

A very heavenly resilience must be transmuted to abused children with narcissistic, psychopathic mothers who are just crazy enough to be so jealous of an infant as to inflict all kinds of torture. She knew God had given her the blessing of a certain toughness of spirit, because as the doctor left the room he quipped, "I'm surprised you survived and are still alive."

—*Dianne Irwin*

THE ENIGMA

MY STORY BEGAN IN 1965 when I was five years old. My mother married my stepfather then and I have no memories before that year.

The first two things I vividly remember about anything are the beatings my stepfather gave me and his overpowering, acrid smell.

My mother never tried to protect me and in my child's mind, I thought I knew why. I thought if she tried to shield me from his abuse that she would get hurt, too. I thought we were sufferers together, trying to survive my stepfather's wrath. I believe I thought that because, as a child, it was easier and more natural to believe rather than think that she simply didn't care.

After I was grown, I asked her if he ever hit her and she replied, "Oh, he KNEW better."

Part of me died inside when she said that because in that instant I knew she was never afraid to intervene, she simply didn't care.

She always seemed happy when I was a child and I couldn't understand what I thought was the abuse of us both, yet she thrived and I couldn't. It was like I didn't even exist except for the sole purpose of his abuse.

As I grew older I saw that my situation was very different from that of other children. I saw mothers (and fathers, gasp!) being affectionate with their children.

I longed for and craved this affection so much the pain was palpable.

I knew that my stepfather was a monster but I didn't understand what my mother was. She was an enigma to me, always keeping herself at an emotional distance from me yet I desperately craved her love.

At the time, I never felt bitter or angry that she didn't protect me from him, just very sad for us both because I thought she must be in some way like me, scared and abused.

The beatings my stepfather inflicted upon me were viscous. He used electrical cords, belts, and his fists.

I first tried to commit suicide when I was eight years old. I would sneak large rocks into my bedroom and at night when I was alone, I would hit myself in the head thinking that if I could just hit myself hard enough, I would die. I tried this many times during my eighth year. I tried again when I was ten. My stepfather told me to go get the belt, and I couldn't stand one more beating. Something came over me, some kind of blind form of desperation and I went to get the belt but I ran out the back door instead. I kept running until I came to the highway, US1, and I kept running. I had found another way to die that I was sure would work and I ran straight into traffic. Cars were dodging me and going off to the side of the road and into the median. I could not get a car to hit me. I then ran to some old houses on the other side of the highway, not knowing if they were occupied or not and banged on all their doors and windows screaming "Help me, please help me," but no one answered their door. After a few hours I didn't know what else to do so I went back. I was beaten savagely and then told that they both had done me this huge favor because they hadn't called the police because they would have come and arrested me for being a runaway and then I would have been in jail for a long time. I was ten years old; I believed them.

One night at church, I had a part in a play. I was up on the stage when I noticed my mother furiously motioning something to me. What happened was my costume had slipped up and my bloody welts were showing. She was trying to get me to adjust it where they didn't show.

Once, after I was grown, I asked my mother why she didn't give me to my natural father when they divorced when I was four. She replied, "I didn't want to give him the satisfaction of having you." Part of me died a little more right then because I could have had a wonderful life had he raised me. I met him when I was grown and he is a kind, funny and compassionate man.

Besides the beatings, my stepfather had a particular way to torture me. Every day at dawn, I had to put on my "work clothes" and go outside and clear property with a pick ax, a regular ax and a shovel. Sometime I had to move cement blocks long distances from one place to another. If I didn't work well enough or fast enough, another beating ensued. I remember after being beaten, how badly the cuts and welts burned when my sweat would get into them as I continued to work. Summers were my own private hell. There was no school to break up the abuse, and every day at dawn, I had to get up and put on my "work clothes" and go outside and clear property or whatever else he contrived for me to do, until the sun went down. When I was allowed to come inside, my mother would bandage my bloody hands and I was sent back out. Every day of "summer vacation."

I still hate summer.

After I had grown, I would spend what little money I had on a Greyhound bus and wonderful presents to try to make every holiday special, like a real family time, maybe for some love.

One Christmas morning, after having spent all night on a bus guarding presents, I called my mother when I arrived at the station. When she answered the phone, I said, "Merry Christmas! Good morning!" Her reply was a harsh "What's so good about it."

Without fail, every holiday after presents had been opened, she would say to me in hate, "You went overboard with the gifts, as usual."

When I was in my twenties something happened that I did not know about until years later. My stepfather decided that he wanted me, but not as a daughter.

My mother's hateful treatment of me compounded exponentially during those years and I was clueless as to why. He never made any advances toward me. Then he did. My mother had taken a job at a retail store and I was there for Christmas. On Monday, she went back to work, and he took his chance. He tried to put his hands on my body, he tried to hold me in an embrace, he tried to kiss me and he told me, "A lot of step-daddies and stepdaughters do it." I called a friend from eight hours away to come get me and I got the hell out of there.

Then I began counseling. I felt like he was trying to destroy the one part of me that he hadn't already destroyed. In time, with therapy, I slowly began to put the ugly puzzle together, no matter how badly I didn't want to see the whole picture. I began to understand that my mother, who was such an enigma to me when I was a child, was actually a narcissist, abusive by neglect, and a hateful woman who just didn't have it in her being to love me.

I am now 55 years old and I finally went no contact with my mother just three months ago.

I cut the IV line that was poisoning my soul. I feel better every day. I survived. I want to see the sun and smell the flowers. I survived and I want to live.

—*Tammie Goodell*

WAITING FOR SWEET AIR

NIGHTS ARE THE WORST.

I am a dedicated father of a 16-year-old girl. I adore her and miss her terribly, but despite my best efforts, I have seen her only twice in four years.

Those two occasions were normal and loving. Absolutely nothing adds up, except parental alienation syndrome. It is apparent that my fears during a decade of hostile, aggressive parenting by the mother and stepfather have been realized.

I believe my daughter has been damaged by very subtle parental alienation and by the not so subtle manipulation and litigious ways of the narcissistic alienating parent. I have become much too familiar with the debilitating feelings of betrayal, treachery, loss, false accusation, gender bias, ignorance, injustice, and reckless indifference.

In the daytime I often find that my parental alienation–affected daughter crosses my thoughts. Not once or twice, but scores of times every day. I find that my parental instincts shackle me and the feelings of helplessness that I constantly endure leave me living my life in limbo. I can't not be a father, but I am also prevented from being a father.

Negative emotions thrive in this state of limbo. After years of suffering, I have managed reasonably successfully to summon my brain to quickly and forcibly lock down the gates to those negative thought pathways. It's always very tempting to entertain melancholy thoughts about her, what she may be doing and how it will be when things are right again. I am certain she will be in my life again, but what really scares me is that I was equally as certain that this could never happen to us.

Gotye sang, "You can get addicted to a certain kind of sadness" and I knew that observation all too well. Like most addictions, there's a heavy price to pay. In this kind of emotional roller-coaster existence I have learned that if I let melancholy in the door, it is never a quick indulgence. Very quickly it unmasks itself as self-pity and knows all the shortcuts in my brain to the place labeled

"Soul Destroying Heartache." Likewise, nostalgia is now an unwelcome guest in my thoughts because it too knows how to get in the door and then wreck the joint.

So in my waking hours, I have learned to cope by trying to keep my mind busy in the present. I focus on the many good things that I am lucky to have in my life. But try as I might, I have not reclined into an admirable Buddhist discipline of living in the moment. It's more like I have chosen to wear blinders, because if I let my mind relax into idle thought, as sure as the sun rises, there will be my little girl on my mind and I will once again be searching for sense out of senselessness, reason out of chaos and justice where there is none.

I allow myself to daydream about the future, but the past is now too painful, too sure to bring back the familiar feeling of being kicked in the stomach for just trying my hardest to be her dad and be in her life.

That's why the nights are the worst. All the emotions I suppress in daylight come out at night in my mind. There's no conscious distraction I can use to keep the demons at bay. Sometimes I awake from a shaking nightmare, my whole being strangled in angst. I never had nightmares before this constant grieving for my daughter. There's something very unnatural about grieving for a child you know is alive and well who may or may not resume her rightful place in your life at any moment.

At other times I awake suddenly in the dead of night with my mind racing, trawling desperately for answers to questions that I have already asked a thousand times. Why? What else can I try?

This is the existence of an alienated parent. Unless you have been through it you will never know the constant gnawing agony. Perhaps this may help you understand us more.

I draw strength from a quote by Richard Nixon: "The greatness comes not when things go always good for you. The greatness comes when you're really tested. When you take some knocks, some disappointments. When sadness comes. Because only if you've been in the deepest valley can you know how magnificent it is to be on the highest mountain."

I now spend most of my time climbing out of the valley with a new partner in life whose heart bursts with compassion and selflessness. But I'll never really scale the heights again until my child finds her way back, whether that takes another day, another year, or the rest of my life.

She knows my door never closes. There are no guarantees in this twilight world of sabotaged attachment strings, but I have optimism that she will find her way back. She may nervously peer inside or she may just knock the door off its hinges.

When she does, I will be grateful. I will dwell on that highest mountain. I will drink in the rarified air and be content, because we can only really appreciate the sweetness in life after we have truly tasted the bitterness.

—Steve B.

THE UNWANTED KISS

EACH TIME THE POSTMAN DELIVERED one more discreet white envelope addressed to me, an adult married woman, I was reminded of the innocence of a child and that unwanted kiss. I needed for this undesirable mail to stop, but over the years I could not even get my mother's deeply embedded, troubling words to go away. I could still hear her spiteful, cutting voice saying, "It's all your fault."

As a young girl, my mother accused me of giving her cold sores. Supposedly, I gave her an unwanted kiss. Since I don't remember her ever holding me, it's hard to picture myself giving her a kiss with my sore, infected lips covered in white cod liver ointment. Over the years, my mother often embarrassed me with her need to make someone else pay at any cost for her unfortunate experiences. And I wasn't immune to her revenge. Out of the blue, she would interject into a conversation how, I, her daughter, had doomed her for life with the unwanted kiss. Pointing at me, she would complain, "You know you are the one that gave me cold sores."

As I opened up the discreet white envelopes, I knew where this malicious garbage came from. Someone had been requesting brochures with information on genital herpes from a pharmaceutical drug company to be sent to me on a regular basis: my mother. She had a track record for doing off-the-wall, hurtful things like this. Although the fact that my mother had been an RN for years was supposed to make it the honest-to-goodness truth. I always just ripped the literature into shreds. I've never had genital herpes. She mistakenly believed that cold sores and genital herpes were one and the same. I am sure that my mother must have gotten another cold sore and again wanted to get even with me for giving them to her years ago. I felt ashamed for being the child who had once kissed her.

My husband had never taken a stand with my mother in our marriage of over twelve years, but he was also fed up with her continual nonsense. I was shocked when he took my medical doctor father aside and insisted that the white, discreet envelopes were going to have to stop. My father just shook his head in disbelief and said, "Where did your mom get a crazy idea like that?"

After their brief conversation, the undesirable mail abruptly ended. And oddly enough, my mother didn't make her usual scene as she does when she wants others to think she has been falsely accused. At the time, I didn't know there was an even deeper meaning to my mother's cruel thoughts. For some reason, my mother had a desire to take her vengeance one step further and blame someone else for giving me cold sores in the first place.

I am adopted and several years ago I went searching for my birth mother. Sadly, I learned that she had passed away when I would have been only eight years old. It was no secret that my birth mother had been a 36-year-old promiscuous woman. Ten months after my birth, she got pregnant again from another affair. I couldn't condemn my birth mother for her reckless choices. What I needed from her was to shelter me from my adoptive mother's abuse.

Without a doubt, I believe that my adoptive mother had made some broad assumptions from what limited information she knew about the woman who gave birth to me. Since genital herpes can be passed on to the unborn child, I guess my adoptive mother figured that I had contracted the herpes cold sore virus from her.

Even when I was grown up, my adoptive mother never treated me as an equal. Regretfully, we never enjoyed each other's company as adults. It was as if since childhood there was always this glass between us and I couldn't touch or reach out for her. Through her eyes, I was still the compliant child who she controlled with her harsh words and actions. I don't reveal my personal heartaches as a badge of courage, but instead as a means to share with others a turning point in my life when I started hearing a little girl's innocent voice crying out somewhere inside me.

Even today, as I struggle to push aside my adoptive mother's unkind, painful words so they won't hurt me anymore, I can't help but wonder if she also thinks losing the love of two mothers is in some way "all my fault," that I, the deliverer of an unwanted kiss, was unworthy of their love.

—*JoAnne Bennett*

EULOGY OF DISINHERITANCE

I am everywhere and nowhere.
I am solid and in shreds.
I have no center and in its place
A hole, full of empty, full of dead.

A vacuum, left behind where treasure gleamed,
Displayed as sparkling hope and innocence
Which you, my father, plundered. Again.

Over and over, I opened to you the hidden genius gems
Which might entice you to look
Inside for such compassion that might match for mine,
To find me in yourself and be valued, be loved, be fine.

But what you found so lovely, vulnerable and rare, you stole.
Then you rampaged through the rest.
Pulled out the pieces, declared them cursed, dirty, vile, evil,
That nothing ever was the best.

You came disguised as my father but were the Pirate Beast,
Denying me upon your death
The remainder of my life with peace.

I am here and I am gone. I am built and destroyed.
I am scattered and found, within the ashes of your bones.
I am severed from your name.
I am true and you were lies—
Another gilded promise made.
I am the beneficiary of the gift of empty.
From you, instead.

—*Deb Martens*

MY MOTHER'S VOICE

I WROTE THIS POEM ABOUT hearing my mother's voice in my head and the impact that it has in every part of my life. Her voice stops me from asking for help or healing from the years of abuse. Her voice forces me to set impossible standards for myself that I can never meet. (Her voice is in italics.)

I Can't
Stand to hear your voices
In my
flooded ears
Why do you have to make everyone miserable?
Can't take anymore.
I need silence. I can't think.
I don't know
what I need.
I don't.
You want.
You need.
I give. You take.
You always give them too much because you felt deprived as a child.
Admit it.
I don't have anything to give.
Can't hear you asking.
Can't take care of you.
Go away,
Go
AWAY!
My skin is thin,
holding the shattered pieces,
under
A mosaic of shame and skin
My coworker's daughter slept with her husband. I swear if you sleep with my husband

I'll kill you.

Splinters work their way to the surface, poking through,

Impaling me, holding me prisoner.

I shouldn't have had to give up anything because I had kids.

Your dad is the one

who

left.

Why is this who I am? I don't want to be like this.

Can't stand it, can't stand being in my skin.

Get out,

Get OUT!

What will make this stop?

How do I feel better?

If I could stop

Eating?

Your sister is a clotheshorse.

She can wear anything.

Cutting?

Crying?

Drinking?

Disassociating?

Lying?

Snapping?

Trying?

Everything's always about you, isn't it?

I can't stop.

Nothing is helping.

Maybe I should cut deeper. Last time there was

so much.

Maybe I should throw up my food again.

You shouldn't eat that. It's fattening.

I'm dizzy, I'm tired. I'm useless.

I'm failing them.

Again.

Should I

Swallow the pills?

If you're going to kill yourself do it in your room.

I want to get back in bed.

And never get up.

Who would know? Can I hide it?

I know.

I should ask someone for help.

I should tell someone.

Before it's too late.

I know.

I can't.

The school called. I know you told them your dad hits you.

You just

wait

until I tell him.

No one can know.

Would it be easier for them if I were gone?

It's your fault he left.

Holding back the truth, can't let it out, can't let go.

Just can't.

Can't hide.

Need to hide, desperate to be invisible.

Eyes watching,

Holding

expectation,

disappointments.

Why do you always blame me? I'm the one who

stayed.

I'm not supposed to act this way.

I'm the pretender. I used to be good at faking my life.

Now I'm struggling through seconds,

Losing my fake smile

Fake personality

False relationships built on pretense.

If he's going to live in my house he should pay to sleep with you.

No one knows me. But they think they do.

I used to be so good at this.

What happened?

Who am I?

Losing control

Lost.

I'd do anything.

Do I have to die to make this stop?

You hate me this way.

I hate it all.

I hate you.

I hate them.

I hate me. More.

This is wrong. This is sick.

I'm sick.

You're always sick. You just want attention.

Get help. Get help.

There's no help.

No one can help. Nothing can help.

Why are you trying to make your issues my problem? Not everything is about you.

I have a life to live.

How did I end up back here?

Again and again.

Here

I

Am

Should I give up?

It always comes back to this.

I don't want this.

My children were always last after the horses and my husband.

I don't feel guilty.

I'm a weight dragging them down.

He'll use this later if I show how bad it is.

Who would take care of them if I'm not here?

Someone needs to protect them.

This isn't for them.

How do I keep them from

Seeing this?

I wanted to be good at this.

I wanted

I'm not.

You never call me. You don't care

about me.

Is your sister home? Where does she live?

Tell her to call me.

I'll help

her.

I just want this to be over.

How do I get well?

I have to think.

Can't.

He always said she didn't

care

About anyone.

But herself.

—P. J. Ward

GIRL UNWANTED

I SPENT MY WHOLE CHILDHOOD with a mum and dad who were both NPD (narcissistic personality disorder). They divorced when I was four. None of my childhood was about me, but rather all about the dysfunction they inflicted on me, with them playing constant victim, while my needs or feelings were punished.

My mother hated me due to my independence even as a child. I was independent due to being neglected, so it was a catch-22. She was resentful of my needs as her child, and my brother was the golden child. My mother married three times and had many boyfriends. She subjected us to trauma and instability and we had no voice to express our experiences.

I was molested by multiple family members, including my father. We experienced traumas like a man shooting himself in the head in our lounge room. My mother made me wear clothes that smelt like death. I slept in a urine-soaked bed every night as punishment for wetting the bed. I was told I was a pig with food and I developed an eating disorder at nine years old.

My mother was cold, cruel, and manipulative. A real mommy dearest. She tricked everyone into thinking she was just a struggling single mum doing her best.

I was locked in my room for days at a time as punishment. Now as an adult I spend most of my time alone in my room. I developed an imaginary life in my head and pretended my life was whatever was good on TV. Now TV is my comfort, my security blanket.

I grew up never complaining. I spent my childhood going hungry, being cold, and turning mute through out primary school so that I didn't "bother" anyone. Every interaction with my mother was cold, prickly, and terrifying. My brother was always carrying out cruelty that my mother encouraged on her behalf. He was treated completely different than I and could do no wrong.

From a young age I was running my family home, cooking and cleaning. If I didn't do the dishes then I ended up with dirty dishes on my bed. I had no childhood. We were also poor. My father was all about appearances and only used me for his sexual attraction to young girls. As an adult he was arrested for child pornography. He's a gambler and an alcoholic. When I outed the abuse as an adult in my 30s, I was attacked by every single family member, who were all instructed by my parents as the smear campaign began.

It's been eight years since I've implemented no contact. Yes, I'm free, but still damaged from a childhood spent feeling like I don't belong, rejected by my family. I'm independent and find it hard to rely too much on others or bond with people consistently. I'm in my shell most of the time.

I'm married with two adult sons who are my world. I'm a gentle, kind and caring person with so much compassion for others. I believe my deep empathy was formed in response to my own suffering. I don't think about these traumas anymore. If I do it's fleeting.

My life is mine and I'm not going to live in a prison of trauma. My self-imposed isolation is no longer a punishment, but rather it is my sanctity. I'm all right. I survived. I'm free.

—*Dyan Linley Moore*

ABOUT THE AUTHOR

BREE BONCHAY is a licensed psychotherapist (LCSW). Though trained as a general practitioner, she has narrowed her scope to relationships. She holds a bachelor's degree in journalism with a minor in psychology from California State University, Northridge, and a master's degree in clinical social work from the University of Southern California.

Specializing in helping people recover from narcissistic abuse and toxic relationships, she blogs regularly on the topic of narcissism and is the founder of the Narcissistic Abuse and Toxic Relationship Forum on Facebook. She has a psychotherapy and consulting private practice in Los Angeles and has appeared on radio as a guest expert.

Her biggest accomplishment, however, is having raised a wonderful teenage daughter. In her spare time, she enjoys hiking with her "other child," (her Labrador), traveling, decorating, and working on her second book, about how to move on after narcissistic abuse, titled "Stover" (So Totally Over!).

You can connect with Bree via her website, http://narcabuse.com, follow her blog at http://relationshipedia.me, or join her Facebook community at Narcissistic Abuse and Toxic Relationship Forum, http://facebook.com/narcopath.

SUBMIT YOUR STORY

If you're interested in submitting your story for consideration in the second edition of *I Am Free*, visit http://iamfreestory.com for submission guidelines.

ABOUT THE CONTRIBUTORS

Jessica Ayres graduated valedictorian from Delaware County Community College with an associate's degree in communications. She then went on to graduate magna cum laude with a bachelor of arts degree in broadcasting, telecommunications, and mass media from Temple University in Philadelphia, Pennsylvania. Along with being a research analyst in competitive intelligence for the pharmaceutical industry, Jessica owns and operates her own small, fair-trade, eco-friendly jewelry company called "Je Suis." When she is not actively serving as a den leader for the Cub Scouts pack in her area, Jessica enjoys kickboxing, hiking, gardening and spending time with her five-year-old son. At present, Jessica is writing a memoir regarding her and her son's journey through his diagnosis of sensory processing disorder, ADHD, and autism.

Steve B. is a firefighter and father in Australia. He is waiting to reunite with his daughter, and his blog can be found at http://sb393.wordpress.com.

Chantal Cayce is an American writer, filmmaker, actress, and lifelong metaphysician. While she regards the experience described in this story as the most traumatic of her life, as an artist, she has been aware from earliest consciousness that Everything is Material, more grist for the mill. Chantal feels grateful that she has gained access to a new emotional palette of colors she never previously knew existed, which have been added to her constant process of the alchemical transmogrification of pain and joy into art.

Kelsey Chizmar will finish her bachelor of arts degree in applied psychology in December 2016. Following that, she will be attending graduate school to become a psychologist. She offers reassurance and support to anyone suffering through a tough time like this and can be contacted through Instagram and Twitter @kelseyyyychizmar. She enjoys running half marathons and spending time with loved ones.

Chloe is a media arts Graduate and mother of three. Her passion has always been in the creative field.

Kerrie Lee Clayton received her bachelor of music in music therapy from East Carolina University and her master of divinity from Campbell University Divinity School. She serves as a full-time minister of music at First Baptist Church in Smithfield, North Carolina. She has two stepchildren that she has always and will always consider like her own but as expected, she has been forbidden from continuing to be part of their lives through visits, phone calls, or cards. To aid the healing process after being married to a narcissist, she is helping children through the local foster care system and is planning to begin working on her doctorate in education in the fall of 2016. She also hopes to write a book one day about how theology shapes abusers and their victims.

Ashley Dunn, DVM, is the Medical Director and veterinarian at an emergency exclusive veterinary practice in the Lakes Region of New Hampshire. She earned her veterinary degree from the Virginia-Maryland Regional College of Veterinary Medicine and her undergraduate degree from St. Mary's College of Maryland. Before that, she grew up on the Eastern Shore of Maryland. When she isn't saving dogs and cats or spending time with her two children, she is also a crocheter, a figure skater, and a Dave Matthews Band fan.

A. P. Heart began writing about narcissistic abuse in late 2014 after determining the woman of his dreams, his soon-to-be ex, displayed narcissistic traits. This was only discovered as a result of investigating his codependent behaviors that were identified as a result of counseling. He began writing a blog called Aprehensiveheart at http://aprehensiveheart.wordpress.com, where he writes about his experiences prior to, during, and after his divorce from his narcissistic wife. He provided a running time line of his story and how he copes (or doesn't cope) with things that have and are occurring in his life.

Alice Isak spent the first half of her adulthood as an educator, including work as a high school English teacher, adjunct writing professor, early literacy tutor, and curriculum writer. While she is still deciding what her life's second act will involve, she is already certain that commitments to social justice and to experimental cake-baking will each play a significant part. Alice shares a creaky-floored but spaciously windowed apartment with two aging cats, who tolerate her reasonably well (though they would prefer if her culinary adventures involved more cheese and less lemon). A poet and memoirist, Alice's current academic interest is in how survivors of trauma can use writing as a tool in their recovery. She blogs about her own recovery from narcissistic family systems and relationships, as well as other topics, at http://coffeeandablankpage.com.

Lindsay J. is thankful for her the opportunity to share her story and hopes that her words can help others. After many failed relationships with abusive narcissists, she has finally found peace on her own. She has started over more times than she would care to admit but would do it all over again in order to be free. She doesn't know exactly what she wants yet but is certain of what she doesn't want in her life. Lindsay has lived without regrets and is determined to learn from each and every experience.

Hope Jay is an attorney practicing family law and matrimonial law. She also has a master's in social work and she is an aspiring novelist. Hope advocates daily in the court system for victims of domestic violence and narcissistic abuse. As a survivor of narcissistic abuse herself, she is uniquely able to understand and assist clients as they navigate the challenges of the court system. Hope is determined to make changes through her legal work and advocacy to bring to light the effects of the insidious psychological and emotional abuse on victims in child custody cases where NPD is involved. She also facilitates a support group for survivors of intimate partner violence. Hope's greatest accomplishment is being a mother to two intelligent and beautiful teenage daughters. You can visit Hope's blog at http://hopejaylaw.com.

Lynette Johnson is a graduate of Weber State University with a BA in history. She currently works at Brigham Young University. Lynette is the proud mother of three children and grandmother to one child. She enjoys spending time with her family and traveling. She has been a strong advocate promoting the awareness of narcissistic abuse since her divorce in 2009 from a narcissist. She is currently working on an autobiography about her experience. She also is actively working toward legislative change for children who suffer narcissist abuse by a parent. Currently, Lynette has created a board on Pinterest, which includes pins on education on narcissism, humor, and motivational support for suffers of narcissistic abuse. Her board can be found at http://pinterest.com/lynettej1/dealing-with-a-narcissistic-ex/.

Mary Laumbach-Perez received her bachelor of arts in sociology and is enrolled in a master of science program. Mary is an educational advocate for students with special needs/disabilities. Mary provides pro bono advocacy work to low-income families throughout New Jersey. Mary is a public speaker and offers workshops on disabilities to parent groups and has presented at state conferences. Professionally, Mary is a nationally certified employment services provider (CESP) with 10 years of experience working with the developmental disabilities and special education population. She is employed full time as an administrator for a young adult program at a private special education school. For her disabilities advocacy work, Mary is a recipient of the 2015 New Jersey Passaic County Champions for Disabilities award, received a New Jersey Senate and General Assembly Citation and is a recipient of the "Best Blogs of 2014" for ADHD World Awareness Month. Mary enjoys photography, hiking, writing, and yoga in her spare time. She is currently writing a disabilities awareness and advocacy book about her life experiences. She has two sons and resides in New Jersey. Mary's favorite quote is from Martin Luther King Jr.: "Our lives end the day we become silent on issues that matter."

Deb Martens passionately supported learning-disabled students, those with a history of complex behavior issues, and blind children and was a braillist in the education system for many years until multiple sclerosis fatigue made it impossible for her to continue working. She is a woman with great persistence and the survivor of a first marriage to an abusive narcissist. She very recent realized that her family of origin was not only home to an alcoholic father but hid a lifetime of sixty years with a raging narcissist and two siblings as covert flying monkeys. Deb has two grown children who are also survivors, with healthy relationships and good jobs. Her fierce advocacy for her children in the first marriage and protecting them form a grandparent abuse reinforce for her how important it is to share the truth of our stories.

Kelly Meadows enjoys spending time with her children and writing. She hopes her writing will be helpful and inspiring to others. Kelly plans to continue to write more in the future.

Sabine McCloud is a criminal defense attorney and mother of two. She is recovering from a relationship with a narcissist that lasted 12 years. In her spare time, she enjoys reading and cooking. She especially loves spending time with her two biggest cheerleaders, her children.

Erin McGee is a writer, accidental feminist, and soul-searcher living in New York City. She is not a therapist and did not major in psychology; she is just a woman who fell head over heals in love with a man and married him and then pretty quickly (or much too slowly, depending on your sense of time) realized he was not who she thought he was. She blogs about her divorce and recovery from betrayal and narcissistic/sociopathic abuse at http://oopsimarriedanarcissist.blogspot.com.

Rebecca McGranahan is a 45-year-old psychology student, disability assistant professional, preschool teacher, dancer, narcoleptic (really!), friend, animal lover, and survivor who resides in Long Beach, California. She has two metal hips, a positive attitude, and has not beaten cancer but survived narcissistic abuse. Rebecca spends her time helping others who struggle with disabilities and loves to walk, frolic, dance in the rain, daydream, and enjoy the new life she has given herself by finally being ... free.

Athena Moberg, CPC, is a writer, speaker, and trauma recovery coach to adult survivors of childhood sexual abuse and narcissistic parents. She educates and creates awareness about all forms of abuse and their debilitating aftereffects, while sharing her 40-year battle and recovery journey. Athena is invited to speak at churches and organizations across the United States, courageously uncovering her true life story, which reveals forbidden generational secrets driven by drugs, crime, exploitation, manipulation, and lies. Athena survived being beaten, molested, lent out, traded, given away, and ultimately raised by people who told her she should have never been born. Now enjoying freedom and a rewarding career among practitioners treating those suffering from childhood trauma, she and her business partner facilitate online safe communities where survivors from all over the world come to heal in safety. Athena leads workshops for adults, middle and high school students, and also serves on her church prayer team with a heart for intercessory prayer. She passionately motivates others into a deeper level of faith while encouraging them to love and accept themselves just as they are. Athena resides in Maui, Hawaii, with her wonderful husband of four years. She has one son who is a Marine Corps veteran and a daughter-in-law in veterinary school. Athena's resources may be found online wherever books are sold.

Dyan Linley Moore is married with two adult sons. Due to abuse growing up with a narcissistic mother and father she finished school with a year seven level education. She returned to studies in her twenties to achieve year twelve level of education. She studied welfare in her early twenties and received two certificates in welfare. She worked in the human services field and then furthered her studies by studying psychology for three years at university, all while raising her two young boys. She was determined to educate herself and make the most of her later opportunity in education. Dyan believes her interests in helping others came from her abusive childhood, which helped her heal from the traumas of her life. After all, she knew the damage that can be done by having abusive people in your life and the aftereffects from that experience. She herself knew the potential to heal when given better opportunities that can move you forward. Her passion is helping others to find peace again and move forward. It gives meaning to her suffering. She plans to blog and share her journey to hopefully inspire others. You can visit Dyan's blog at http://gumbootdancer. blogspot.com.au. She is active in her community and her interests include psychology, dance, music, and cats. She hopes all readers of this book find validation, comfort, and inspiration.

Barbara Pederson lives on a small ranch in Oregon where she raises geese, chickens, goats, and horses. She received her bachelor of science degree after she retired from the Department of Corrections, where she worked as a corrections officer at Folsom prison. She writes about the importance of localizing our food supply and was partners with a narcissist for 23 years. This event was chronicled in a book that she recently wrote after the breakup titled *Tin Man: Memoirs of a Sociopath*. This book can be found on Amazon at http://amazon. com/gp/product/B017LB1E64.

Rescuing Little L is a survivor of childhood sexual abuse and violence. She blogs about the complexities of recovery, among other topics, using her experience as a counselor, nurse, woman, wife, and mother. Her passions include alternative and energetic healing therapies, knitting, food, and dogs. She lovingly volunteers as a moderator / virtual assistant for several national organizations for trauma survivors. She lives in the St. Louis area with her wildly creative daughter and maintains safe, boundary-controlled relationships with all the narcissists in her life. Rescuing Little L's sites include http://rescuinglittlel. wordpress.com and Facebook: Rescuing Little L.

Joan Rice works in management and is also in the process of getting two degrees to help survivors fight their abusers within the court system. She is also working on getting the first book of a young adult series she created published, along with completing the first manuscript to another young adult series. She is a strong believer in protecting children from these monsters and hopes to stand beside or in front of other survivors, giving them the strength to continue fighting for their children and freedom.

Alexandra Sarell is graduating from Saint Mary-of-the-Woods College in May 2016 with a BS in biology with a focus on environmental biology and minors in business administration and chemistry. She hopes to obtain a master's in dietetics and a master's in fisheries, conservation, and wildlife biology and work as an environmental researcher. She is active in her campus community support in and encouraging her peers to seek the life they want, not to be fearful in the life they have. If you are interested in correspondence, please contact her through her email address at alexandrasarell@gmail.com.

Starlene Schlim is a retired accounting clerk. She has one adult daughter and three granddaughters. Starlene is a frequent blogger. The dark experiences of suicide, addiction, prison, domestic violence, and sexual abuse have touched and devastated her life in one way or another. She is currently compiling her notes, poems, and journal entries for her memoir. Her goal is to reach as many young girls and women as possible in hopes that something they read will ignite a spark of hope and strengthen their resolve to be true to themselves. You can read her story titled "Fear of Abandonment" at http://GoodTherapy.org/blog/understanding-fear-of-abandonment-062914

Shalini Singh, MD, is a medical doctor by profession. She served ten years as a doctor in the army. She has two children. She enjoys writing poetry and is an avid reader.

Ng Jern Siong is an emerging concerned citizen. Having grown up in the small Malaysian town of Taiping, his first shot at the 'big wide world' was when he moved to New Zealand for university study. This move awakened his broader understanding of societal perspectives surrounding LGBT issues and piqued his interest in sharing his own story as well as that of others. To date, Jern has had several of his works published in online platforms and forums. As one of the next generation of social commentators, he will continue to share his stories and observations of the world through print and online media. A graduate in business, with a minor in sexuality studies, Jern plans to pursue his postgraduate work in issues of sexuality and the Asian community.

Emilia Strong is a young woman who enjoys working with people. She lives in the big city but has her heart in the archipelago where she grew up. She loves to travel the world. Today she makes sure to live life to the fullest, even when it's just about laughing her heart out alone on the living room floor. She's made the decision to always believe in love because it's all around and can be found within. One day she hopes to become a therapist, a special ed teacher, author of something empowering, or anything that supports and encourages someone to find their inner strength. She started a blog, Roar in the Afterglow at http://roarintheafterglow.blogspot.fi/ in the summer of 2015. Roar stands for bravery and Afterglow for the glow she still carries from that day when she finally realized that life is beautiful and set herself free.

Dawn Stott is a writer and artist who studied design and multimedia. She grew up in the San Francisco Bay Area and is one of the founding members of Burning Man. Dawn is an avid cook who loves to garden, embroider, and make up-cycled jewelry from watches, old jewelry, and found objects. She is currently writing her first book about a love story that takes place in a cookbook. She maintains blogs and an Etsy shop as follows: The Morning Mirror: Reflections and other illusions, dustycrevice.livejournal.com; Adventures in Kitchen Alchemy, http://indoorgriller.livejournal.com; and Virtual Genius Design, http://etsy.com/shop/VirtualGeniusDesign. You can also find Dawn on Twitter under the user name of @TheDawnStott, where she loves to write humor and thought-provoking quips while exploring the wonders of a 140-character limit.

Tamara Yancosky-Moore is a devoted Christian who lives in Northern California and is the very proud mother of her two young adult sons, Timothy and Joshua, who are her breath and purpose in her life. Tamara was in an abusive relationship with a covert narcissist, and though it was a tragic experience, she looks at the positive side and has found healing in her relationship with Jesus Christ, the strength and joy she gets from her two sons, and also from many friends she has after having been one of the administrators, for several months, on a Facebook narcissist site. Due to having been on this healing site, she still has many friends whom she keeps in touch with, and each understands the other's struggles from having been through abusive relationships. Tamara enjoys expressing her experiences and feelings through poetry and other writings. Feel free to visit her at http://yancoskytamara@yahoo.com.blog.com.

Made in the USA
Middletown, DE
20 May 2016